San Francisco
STREET SECRETS

by David B. Eames

 W9-BXZ-154

Gem Guides Book Co.
315 Cloverleaf Drive, Suite F
Baldwin Park, California 91706

San Francisco Street Secrets. Copyright © 1995 by Gem Guides Book Company. Printed and bound in the United States of America. All rights reserved. No part of this book may be reproduced in any form or by any electronic or mechanical means, including information storage or retrieval systems, without permission in writing from the publisher.

Permission to use quotations from Amelia Ransome Neville's, *The Fantastic City*, has been granted by Houghton Mifflin Company.

Historic photos have been supplied courtesy of:
The Bancroft Collection—University of California, Berkeley
and the San Francisco History Room—San Francisco Public Library

Modern-day photos by author, Copyright © 1994 by David B. Eames

Maps by David B. Eames and John Mayerski

Cover design by Frederick L. Runyon

First Edition 1995

Library of Congress Catalog Card Number: 94-76114

ISBN 0-935182-75-6

Those of you who know Sharon Darr will understand why this book is dedicated to her.

ACKNOWLEDGMENTS

I would like to thank the following people and institutions for their invaluable assistance: Pat Akre of the San Francisco History Room, San Francisco Public Library, who provided patient research of archival photographs; the Bancroft Library, University of California, Berkeley; and in particular, William M. Roberts, Curator of Pictorial Collections; Lauren S. Bahr, Vice President/Editorial Director at P.F. Collier; and Teresa Buswell, Permissions Coordinator at Houghton Mifflin Company.

All books are judged by their cover; I hope this one will be, too. My brother, Frederick L. Runyon, brought extraordinary talents and enthusiasm to the project, and being able to work with him was a very special pleasure for me.

My love and thanks to Joan C. Runyon for wise counsel; to Kevin Ancic for generous and skillful computer support; and to Téa Darr for keeping the secret.

A gathering of notable business figures from San Francisco's early years. All have streets named after them.

Top (from l. to r.):
Talbot H. Green
Sam Brannan

Bottom (from l. to r.):
Jacob P. Leese
Thomas O. Larkin
William D. M. Howard

ABOUT THE AUTHOR

After several visits, David Eames moved to San Francisco from his native Connecticut in 1974. He had questions that are common among new arrivals to the city — Where is the telegraph on Telegraph Hill? Why is there no beach in North Beach? How do you pronounce "Gough"? From such random musings grew the seeds of *Street Secrets*. A B.A. in English from the University of California, Berkeley, helped prepare him for the libarary research the project entailed.

Today David lives with his wife, Sharon, in a house deep in the redwoods of Larkspur, in Marin County, California. He is a carpenter, a photographer, a translator, a gourmet chef, an avid traveler, and a pretty good juggler. *Street Secrets* is his first book.

TABLE OF CONTENTS

Acknowledgments V

About the Author VII

Introduction X

Reading Street Secrets XI

Maps of the City XII

Chapter 1 - *The Explorers* 1

Chapter 2 - *The Settlers* 9

Chapter 3 - *The Americans* 22

Chapter 4 - *Gold* 41

Chapter 5 - *Statehood* 52

Chapter 6 - *The Vigilantes* 66

Chapter 7 - *The Earthquake* 81

Street Walk #1 - 108

Street Walk #2 - 115

Street Walk #3 - 121

Street Walk #4 - 130

Street Walk #5 - 144

Appendix 156

Photo List... 160

Bibliography 163

Index... 165

INTRODUCTION

Early San Francisco grew at an astonishing pace. The 800 residents of 1848 had to play host to 30,000 newcomers that the Gold Rush brought during the next two years. City surveys were conducted without any systematic planning for future growth, and not much thought was given to the names of the streets. By the turn of the century, when San Francisco's population had soared to 300,000, the City had one set of streets and two sets of avenues designated only by numbers. The suffix "South" was added to one set of avenues to distinguish it from the other. As if this weren't confusing enough, San Francisco also had two sets of streets which were named only with letters of the alphabet. So, for example, there was a Fourth Street, a Fourth Avenue, a Fourth Avenue South, an "F" Street, and an "F" Street South.

It wasn't just the residents of San Francisco who were confused. The Post Office was having a nearly impossible time delivering mail to the right address. "Fourth Avenue South, San Francisco" was easily mistaken for "Fourth Avenue, South San Francisco," which was in a completely separate city.

In 1909, Mayor E. R. Taylor appointed a commission to bring some order out of the chaos. The lettered streets were given complete names; e.g. - "A" Street became Anza Street, "B" Street became Balboa, and so on. The numbered avenues that had the suffix "South" were given names instead of numbers; Fourth Avenue South, for example, became David-son Avenue. This left, mercifully, only one set of numbered streets and one set of numbered avenues.

The 1909 Commission recommended about four-hundred changes. It tried to bring about some consistency in the use of "Lane," "Street," "Boulevard," etc. to designate thorough-fares of different sizes, and it followed certain principles in establishing new street names: A street name

> *should have significance. It should mean something or commemorate some character or event. The names of persons are the best street names, especially those of historic or patriotic significance. It is wholly fitting that men who have served their country well, or who have been local pioneers, or who have made their names conspicuously respected in a community, should have them perpetuated in the names of streets . . . California is blessed with a historic background of peculiar interest, romantic and picturesque. It is a distinct asset that we cannot afford to ignore.*

In following these guidelines, the 1909 Commission immortalized the most remarkable men and women in San Francisco's rich and colorful past. That fascinating history is all around us, in the names of the City's streets.

READING "STREET SECRETS"

This book is divided into two parts. Part One contains seven chapters that give an overview of the history of San Francisco as it is reflected in the City's street names. When people who have streets named for them are mentioned in the text for the first time, their names will be in **bold type**.

The second part of *Street Secrets* contains five walks that explore some of San Francisco's historically important neighborhoods. In this section of the book, **bold type** is used to give specific directions or to orient you generally to your surroundings.

If you are curious about the origin of a specific street name, the index will refer you to the place in the text where that person is discussed. Finally, the appendix contains a listing of all the street names covered in the text, as well as the origins of several dozen additional street names.

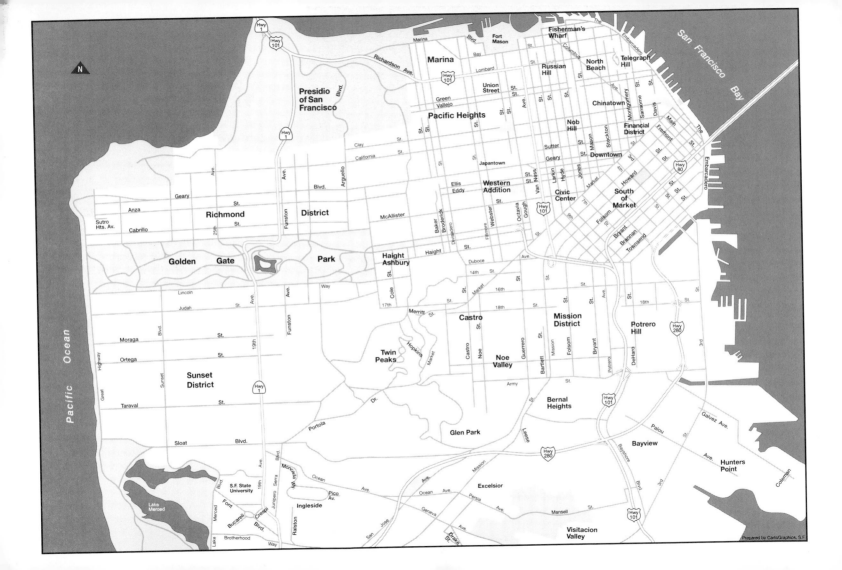

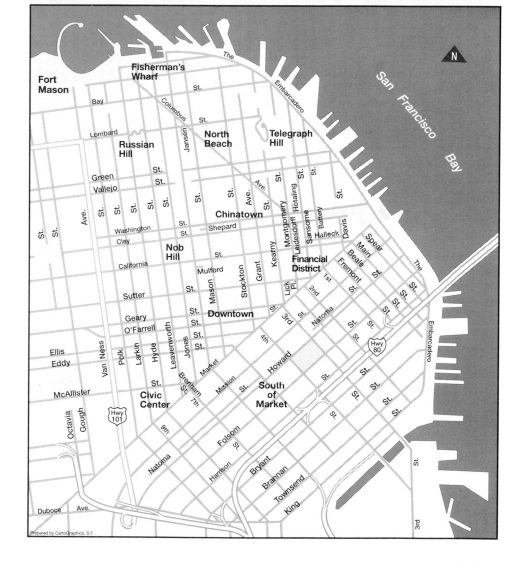

MAPS

The map on the previous page highlights those streets in the San Francisco area that are discussed in the text. Occasionally a street that does not appear in the text will show on the map as a reference point to aid in locating the street under discussion.

The map on this page is an enlargement of the downtown area.

CHAPTER 1

The Explorers

In the summer of 1579, **Francis Drake** was a happy man. He could look back with pleasure on the nearly three years he had spent raiding Spanish shipping along the east and west coasts of the Americas. He had captured the Manilla Galleon, which annually carried gold and silver from Acapulco to the Philippines, and his voyage had been a great success. His exploits, in fact, were to earn him a knighthood from a grateful Queen Elizabeth I when he completed his circumnavigation of the globe. But of his original force of five ships, only the *Golden Hinde* remained. She was overloaded with nearly 30 tons of Spanish treasure, and the seams in her hull were starting to leak badly.

Drake's logbook records that in June he sighted the Farallon Islands, thirty-two miles west of the Golden Gate, (Drake named them the "Islands of Saint James") and that he put into a "convenient and fit harborough" to careen his ship. Drake and his crew received a friendly welcome from the indigenous people, the Coast Miwoks, and for several weeks the English repaired the *Golden Hinde*. When they departed, according to Francis Fletcher, the ship's chaplain and chronicler, they left behind a brass plate

Sir Francis Drake

1

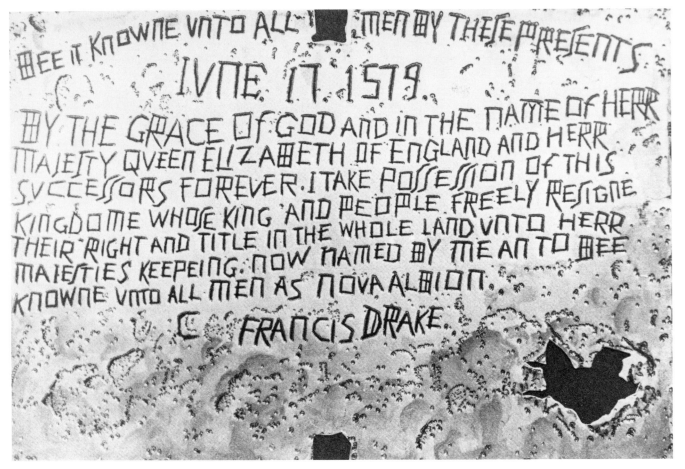

Drake's "Plate of Brasse." The hole at the lower right was for a sixpence coin, which carried the likeness of Queen Elizabeth I.

fixed to a wooden post. On the plate were engraved Elizabeth's name, coat of arms, and claim to all the lands of "Nova Albion."

Imagine the excitement when, in 1936, just such a "Plate of Brasse" was found in Larkspur, in Marin County. For a time it seemed that Drake's landfall must have been in San Francisco Bay, but recent research has thrown the authenticity of the Plate into doubt. The University of California, where the Plate now resides in the Bancroft Library, allowed extensive chemical analyses to be performed. These tests show that the percentages of copper and zinc in the plate do not correspond to those of other brass samples known to be of the period. Furthermore, the edges of the Plate seem to have been cut with a shearing device unknown in Drake's day.

So was Sir Francis Drake the first European to sail into San Francisco Bay? Possibly, though it seems more likely that Drake landed about thirty miles to the northwest, near Point Reyes, where miles of Doveresque cliffs (Drake reported seeing "white bancks and cliffs") might have inspired him to call the land "Nova Albion."

In any event, Drake was certainly not the first European to sail the California coast. In September of 1542, a Portuguese explorer named **Juan Rodrigues Cabrillo** had ventured north from Mexico and had discovered San Diego Bay. Continuing northwards, he sighted Monterey Bay, which he named, *Bahia de Los Pinos*, for the pine trees that grew thickly down to the water's edge. In November he recorded finding the Farallons, yet his log makes no mention of seeing San Francisco Bay. The Golden Gate may have been hidden by fog, or Cabrillo may simply have failed to see it. From a safe distance offshore, where a prudent navigator would stay in unknown waters, the narrow opening is well camouflaged by the backdrop of hills in the landmass beyond. Several later explorers, probably Drake included, sailed past without noticing the Gate.

Between the time of Cabrillo's voyage and the middle of the Eighteenth Century, Spain showed little interest in colonizing Alta California. There are several reasons for this seeming indifference. Rich silver mines discovered in Zacatecas, Mexico, in 1546, drew more attention than the rugged and apparently worthless lands along the California coast. Indian uprisings, beginning with the Mixton War in 1542, made travel through northwestern Mexico dangerous. The main thrust of Spanish North American colonization was concentrated in New Mexico, and the settlements there consumed the limited funds and manpower that were available for empire building.

Other nations did not share the Spanish indifference, however. The Russians, with the encouragement of Catherine II, had extended their otter and seal hunting forays south from Alaska in the early 1760s. The Russian advance was to culminate in the establishment of Fort Bragg in 1812, and their presence there continued until 1841.

Jose de Galvez
Visitador General de Nueva Espana

As a barrier to further encroachment from the north the Spanish resolved to colonize Alta California. **José de Gálvez**, the Spanish Visitador-general, organized a four part expedition, two groups to travel by land and two by sea.

The first of the overland groups was led by **Captain Fernando de Rivera y Moncada,** accompanied by **Father Juan Crespi.** Their band of twenty-five soldiers, forty-two Christianized Indians, and a herd of cattle made the trek in fifty-one days, arriving in San Diego on May 14. The second overland party, led by **Captain Gaspar de Portolá** and **Father Junípero Serra**, reached San Diego July 1.

The march through the deserts of northern Mexico and southern California in summer was a grueling test of endurance, but the sailors fared even worse. Of the two ships, the *San Antonio* made the voyage in fifty-five days and lost none of its crew, though all arrived sick with scurvy. But the *San Carlos*, at one point driven six-hundred miles from shore by contrary winds and currents, sailed for nearly four months before limping into port. According to one report, twenty-four men had died, and the remaining crew were so weakened by scurvy that they couldn't lower a boat.

In spite of these difficulties, Father Serra laid the cornerstone for the first in California's celebrated chain of missions in San Diego, in July 1769. Before his death on August 28, 1784, at age of 70, Serra personally established nine missions. His successors continued the work, and the last of the twenty-one missions was founded in Sonoma in 1823. Serra owes much of his fame to his close associate

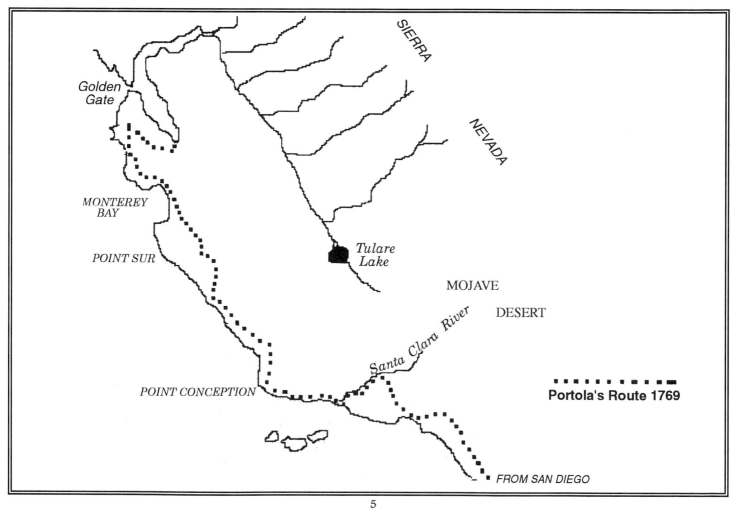

Golden
Gate

SIERRA

NEVADA

MONTEREY
BAY

POINT SUR

Tulare
Lake

MOJAVE

DESERT

Santa Clara River

POINT CONCEPTION

Portola's Route 1769

FROM SAN DIEGO

and biographer, **Father Francisco Palou**, who tended to give him credit which was perhaps due others as well. Today Serra enjoys near mythic status, and no one can claim to be a true Californian until he, or she, can correctly pronounce "Junípero Serra" ("who-KNEE-pair-o SAIR-ra") without obvious exertion.

Father Junipero Serra

Portolá wasted no time in San Diego, he assembled a small party of his healthiest men and continued north along the coast. He hoped to find Monterey Bay, which Sebastian Viscaino, retracing Cabrillo's route in 1602, had touted as a fine harbor. It was hoped that Monterey would be a convenient stop-over point for the Manilla galleons on their return voyages to Acapulco.

The Spanish ships were frighteningly small by today's standards. (The *San Carlos*, for example, was only 58 feet). Every inch of space was packed with precious cargoes, and little room was allotted for the crew's food and water. Much of the impetus for the colonization of Alta California was the desperate need to service the ships. Missions, in addition to converting the native people to Christianity, could provide meat, vegetables, fresh water, and a place for crews to recover from their ordeals. Furthermore, military garrisons, or "presidios," could offer protection from marauding British privateers.

When he reached Monterey, Portolá was confused. He thought he was at the correct latitude, but the bay seen from land appeared much more open than the snug harbor Viscaino had described from his vantage point offshore. To be fair, Portolá was not entirely to blame. Viscaino's description of Monterey as "secure against all winds" certainly overstated matters. In any case, Portolá's confusion proved extremely fortunate, since it caused him to push further north. On October 31 he caught sight of San Francisco Bay for the first time.

Portolá sent a small party ahead under **Sergeant José Francisco de Ortega**, and they reached the Bay on November 2. They determined to reconnoiter as far as *Punta de los Reyes* (Point Reyes), but found their way blocked by the immense estuaries of the northern part of the Bay. After several days were spent trying to get around the barrier, and running low on provisions, Ortega returned to report to Portolá.

It is ironic that both men, having discovered one of the world's greatest natural harbors, felt a keen sense of failure. The Bay was seen not for its enormous potential, but only as an obstacle to further northward progress. To Portolá and Ortega's way of thinking, they had failed. They had seen *Punta de los Reyes*, but had failed to reach it; they hadn't found the "true" bay (i.e. - Drake's Bay) that mariners had reported many years previously; and they had failed to locate Monterey, which had been the goal of their expedition all along. On that note, Portolá and his men retreated to San Diego.

The following year a second Portolá expedition returned to Monterey, more sure of their bearings this time. Serra established the second of the twenty one California missions on June 3, 1770, and the settlement there was secure. Monterey became the seat of power for the Spanish colonies in Alta California and received the lion's share of investment and other support.

Still there was no rush to settle the San Francisco Bay area. A couple of mapping surveys were carried out, including one by Lieutenant Juan Manuel de Ayala, at the helm of

Don Gaspar de Portolá

the *San Carlos*. On August 5, 1775, the durable little ship became the first to enter the Bay (if we discount the *Golden Hinde*). Ayala anchored in the cove, now named for him on the lee side of Angel Island, and recuperated from an accidental gunshot wound he had suffered to his foot. His pilot, José de Cañizares, spent forty-four days exploring the Bay in a longboat and confirmed that it was a harbor in its own right and not connected to Drake's Bay.

Ayala, who curiously has no street named for him in San Francisco, gave names to many of the Bay's geographical features, including several islands. One was Angel Island: *Isla de Nuestra Señora de Los Angeles*. Another, a barren, rocky outcropping, he named for the many pelicans that roosted on it: *Isla de los Alcatraces*, now called Alcatraz Island. Cañizares also named a larger island near the mainland *Isla del Carmen*. At various times this island was called Bird Island, Goat Island, and finally Yerba Buena Island.

The names of the early explorers have a certain romance and mystique to them, and many have been used for street names. Gaspar de Portolá is remembered in Portola Drive, which begins at the end of Market Street, near the top of Twin Peaks. Sir Francis Drake, who may have been the first European to see the Bay, somehow got relegated to a tiny, three-block-long street that lies hidden in the shadow of the Cow Palace. The 1909 Commission used many of the Spanish explorers' names for streets that had previously been designated only with letters of the alphabet. Galvez and Palou replaced Avenues "G" and "P" in the Bayview district. Cabrillo, Ortega, and Rivera are found in the Richmond and Sunset districts, where streets cross avenues in alphabetical order to the north and south of Golden Gate Park. Many people have wondered why these streets are named in alphabetical order. The answer is that they were already known by letters of the alphabet when the 1909 Commission gave them their full names. Sensibly, the Commission assigned them names which kept the order that residents were accustomed to.

By 1775, the Bay had been explored and mapped, but still there was no push by the Spanish to secure claim to their northernmost discoveries by establishing settlements. The era of the settlers would have to wait another year.

Alcatraz as seen from North Point, 1866

CHAPTER 2
The Settlers

By September 1775, the Spanish had finally realized that unless they acted decisively, the English or the Russians were likely to claim Alta California. That month, approval for a major colonizing expedition was granted by the new Viceroy, who gloried in the name of **Lieutenant General Baylio Fray Don Antonio María Bucareli y Ursua.**

Bucareli ordered **Captain Juan Bautista de Anza** to lead two-hundred-and-fifty men and women from the presidio of Tubac, in present-day southern Arizona, overland to Monterey. Perhaps as important as the settlers themselves was the herd of cattle they brought with them. As the herd grew, it became the basis of an active hide and tallow trade, which was the mainstay of Alta California's early economy.

Captain Juan Bautista de Anza

After leading a colonizing expedition of two-hundred-and-fifty men and women from the presidio of Tubac, in present-day Southern Arizona, overland to Monterey, California, Anza and a small group departed almost immediately for the Bay of San Francisco. He arrived at the tip of the peninsula, near present-day Fort Point, on March 28, 1776.

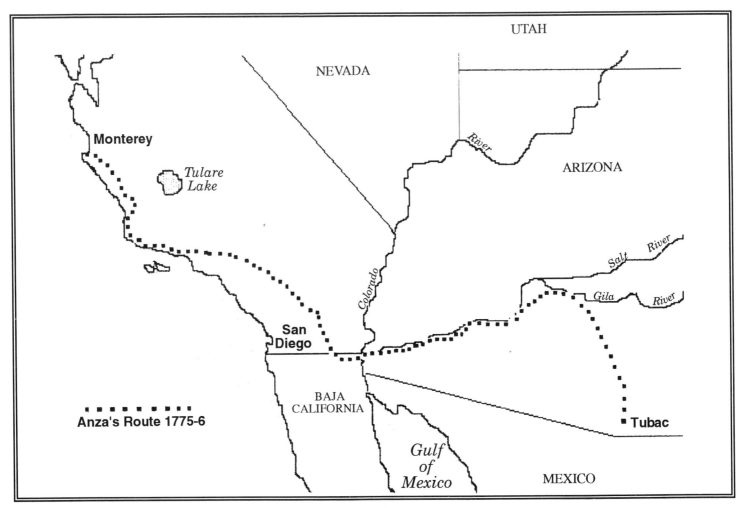

UTAH

NEVADA

ARIZONA

Monterey

Tulare Lake

Salt River

Gila River

Colorado

San Diego

BAJA CALIFORNIA

Tubac

Gulf of Mexico

MEXICO

■ ■ ■ ■ ■ ■ ■ ■
Anza's Route 1775-6

Anza's party had the services of several Indian guides, including **Sebastian Taraval**, who had traveled earlier with the first Portolá Expedition. When Anza's group neared the present U.S.-Mexico border Taraval started to recognize the correct route, which was tremendously encouraging. Moreover, he was able to find natural wells and springs in areas where no other water was available.

Also traveling with Anza was a Franciscan missionary, **Father Pedro Font**. Font was a man of many talents, a mathematician, musician, and geographer; his skills included the use of compass, quadrant, astrolabe, and other navigational devices of the day. With the help of Font and Taraval, and a large measure of good fortune, Anza reached Monterey.

Anza was by all accounts a tactful and capable leader, though perhaps a little proud and overly concerned with the honors due him as an explorer. After his exploits in Alta California he went on to serve as governor of New Mexico. Sadly, he was dismissed from that post for failing to anticipate an uprising by the supposedly "pacified" Yuma Indians. The Spanish Governor General of Northern Provinces, Felipe de Neve, even ordered Anza to stop calling himself the discoverer of the land route to Alta California. De Neve claimed that Anza had merely followed Taraval, but that

disappointing chapter lay some years ahead. In March of 1776, Anza's star was still on the ascendant. He had gotten his colonists safely to Monterey, and an even greater triumph lay before him.

Almost immediately upon arriving in Monterey, Anza and a small group left for the Bay of San Francisco and arrived at the tip of the peninsula, near present-day Fort Point, on March 28, 1776. Before leaving the area, they planted a cross to mark the site for the Presidio. About three miles to the south-east a second cross was placed near a good source of water and pasturage. Since the group had found the stream on the Friday before Palm Sunday (in Spanish, "*Viernes de Dolores*" or "Friday of Sorrows") they called it *Arroyo de Nuestra Señora de Los Dolores*. This was to be the site of the Mission San Francisco de Asís, or as it is now popularly know, Mission Dolores.

Three months later a party led by Anza's second-in-command, **Lieutenant José Joaquín Moraga**, found both crosses still standing. Father Palou celebrated Mass at the Mission site beneath a crude shelter of tree branches on June 29, 1776, five days before the signing of the Declaration of Independence on the other side of the continent.

Construction of the Mission we see today began April 25, 1782. When work was completed nine years later, the building was one-hundred-fourteen feet long, twenty-two feet wide, and had adobe walls four feet thick. Though the parish church (a later addition) was destroyed in the 1906 earthquake and had to be rebuilt, the Mission itself survived with only minor damage. Mission Dolores is thus the oldest building in San Francisco, and is well worth a visit. A small museum houses the baptismal register (more than 28,000 baptisms have been performed here), and an adjacent cemetery is the final resting place for many early settlers who are remembered in San Francisco street names.

With the establishment of the Mission and the Presidio, the City by the Bay had a foothold, albeit a tenuous one, on its sandy, fog-shrouded peninsula. Father Pedro Font, looking out over the water on that fateful March 28, wrote in his journal:

Indeed, although in my travels I saw very good sites and beautiful country, I saw none which pleased me so much as this. And I think that if it could be well settled like Europe there would not be anything more beautiful in all the world, for it has the best advantages for founding in it a most beautiful city . . .

This 1870 photograph of Mission Dolores shows the cemetery where Luis Antonio Arguello, Francisco de Haro, and other notables are buried.

Mission Dolores, at left, and parish church

The new colony on the shores of San Francisco Bay followed the Spanish pattern of development, a cooperative venture of military and religious interests. Presidios protected missions, which in turn became the focal point of surrounding communities.

Beyond their initial investment, the Spanish government offered little support for their fledgling colonies in Alta California. Even with the great natural harbor which the Bay provided, the Spanish presence was precarious. The supply routes from Mexico were long and difficult; there were no signs of gold or silver; and the Indians of the area, to the Spanish way of thinking, were poor and backward.

The first non-Spanish ship to enter the Bay was the *Discovery*, in November 1792, commanded by the great English navigator, George Vancouver. His journal underscores the Spanish policy of neglect. Vancouver found the Presidio manned by only thirty-five soldiers, and its defenses were laughably inadequate. He noted only one cannon, "a brass three-pounder mounted on a rotten carriage." There had been a second cannon, Vancouver was told, but it had exploded recently during a practice firing.

It later became a sore point for the Spanish that they were unable to stop the ever-increasing numbers of foreign visitors. One report to the Viceroy complained: "Confident that there is nobody to restrain them, they come with arrogant boldness to anchor in our very harbors."

Things had hardly improved thirty-four years later, when another English ship, the *Blossom*, called for supplies. Captain Frederick William Beechey feared that Spanish guns would blow him out of the water as he passed through the Golden Gate. He needn't have worried. The Presidio's defenders could do nothing as he ignored their orders to heave to and sailed calmly to an anchor at Yerba Buena cove.

Beechey's report of the *Blossom's* three-year voyage, which runs to two heavy volumes, had this to say about the Presidio:

> *[The Commandante's] house was in a corner of the Presidio, and formed one end of a row, of which the other was occupied by a chapel; the opposite side was broken down, and little better than a heap of rubbish and bones, on which jackals, dogs, and vultures were constantly preying; the other two sides of the quadrangle contained storehouses, artificers' shops, and the gaol, all built in the humblest style with badly burned bricks.*

Don Luís Antonio Argüello held the unenviable position of Presidio Commander from 1787 to 1806. Argüello deserves more sympathy than blame for the sorry state of things. Morale was terrible among his men, who were unhappy to be posted to this lonely limit of empire, and unhappier still when their pay reached them months or even years overdue. Relations with the padres at the Mission, on whom the garrison was dependent for its food, were frequently strained. In spite of all this, Argüello was very gracious to the seal and otter hunters, whalers, and other rugged travelers who occasionally happened by. Vancouver, for example, reported "a very cordial reception and hearty welcome."

In 1806, when the Russian chamberlain, Nikolai Petrovich Rezanov, arrived, he was greeted warmly and invited to share the few comforts that the Presidio had to offer. Rezanov was on a desperate search for food and supplies for the beleaguered Russian colony at Sitka. He inquired urgently if the Comandante could spare any provisions. Don Antonio answered that, regrettably, he could not, since trade with non-Spanish elements was strictly forbidden.

But Rezanov was a persistent fellow, and he continued to plead his case. Coincidentally, he made the acquaintance of Argüello's 15-year-old daughter, Concepción. There are two ways of looking at what happened next. One, the ruthlessly anti-romantic view, says that Rezanov succeeded in extracting the supplies from Captain Argüello by cynically manipulating the affections of the innocent daughter. The second view, while conceding that Rezanov eventually left with his supplies, maintains that he and Doña Concepción fell genuinely (perhaps even instantly) in love.

A novel by Gertrude Atherton and a poem by Bret Harte steer the latter course, which continues along a fairy tale plot line. Rezanov and Concepción get engaged. As a Russian Orthodox member of the royal court, he must travel all the way back to Moscow to secure the Czar's permission to marry a Spanish Catholic. He promises to hurry; she promises to wait.

And then the years go by. Nearly forty years pass with no word of Rezanov. Doña Concepción languishes, but her fidelity is unshakable. Finally the night arrives when she will learn the fate of her fiancé, but the way it is revealed to her is cruel indeed. Sir George Simpson of the Hudson's Bay Company is visiting the Presidio and having dinner at the same table with Concepción and other guests. He entertains them with a curious story he once heard, the story of a Russian chamberlain who had fallen in love with a Catholic foreigner. Seems he needed to get the Czar's permission to marry her, but as he was hastening through the taiga to Moscow he was thrown from his horse and died:

Quickly then cried Sir George Simpson:
"Speak no ill of him, I pray.
He is dead. He died, poor fellow, forty
years ago this day,
Died while speeding home to Russia,
falling from a fractious horse.
Left a sweetheart, too, they tell me.
Married, I suppose, of course!"

City archives record that Argüello Boulevard, which winds through the Presidio and then runs south to Golden Gate Park, is officially named in honor of Don Luís Antonio Argüello. Less officially, it also preserves the memory of Concepción, the beautiful young woman who never stopped waiting for the man she loved.

Mexican independence from Spain brought about the transfer of government in California in 1822. At that time, there were perhaps 3,500 European settlers in all of Alta California. They could no longer count on the support, however lackadaisical, of the Iberian colossus, and became merely a remote outpost of a newly independent, preoccupied and destitute republic. New forms of self-government were needed.

The Mexican administration consisted of an *alcalde* (roughly equivalent to mayor) and a town council, or *ayuntamiento*. **Francisco de Haro** received a majority of the twenty-seven votes cast in the first election, in December, 1834, and became alcalde. The pueblo of Yerba Buena (as distinct from the settlements at the Mission and Presidio) was to grow up along the shores of the Cove, near Yerba Buena Island. It was a natural choice; mariners since Ayala had seen that the Cove offered an excellent anchorage, and fresh water was available in the area.

The first settler was **William Richardson**, who made a rough sketch for the pueblo and petitioned the Mexican authorities to grant him a parcel of land there. Richardson had arrived in 1822 on the whaling ship, *Orion*, which he deserted. He adopted the Spanish ways and language, converted to Catholicism (at least nominally) and married María Martínez, daughter of Presidio Comandante (and later alcalde) Ignacio Martínez. Richardson set himself up as the first harbor master and pilot of San Francisco Bay. He also bought cattle hides and tallow from ranches in the inland valleys and sold them to the trading ships that were increasingly calling at the port.

Richardson was in the right business at the right time. In the Mexican period some 50,000 to 80,000 hides were shipped from California annually, many of them to shoe factories in Massachusetts. The hides were an important medium of exchange in an economy that was still largely based on barter. They became known as "California bank notes," and were worth about two dollars each. By the late 1830s Richardson was a prosperous member of the Mexican establishment, with his hide-and-tallow business, a boat-building enterprise, and a land grant of 19,000 acres in southern Marin county.

Richardson was also granted the much smaller parcel of land he had asked for in Yerba Buena. In 1835 he built the town's first house, four redwood posts set in the sand ground and covered with sailcloth. A few rough boards completed the structure, which was located at what is now 823-827 Grant Avenue, on the west side of Grant, near Clay Street. Two years later Richardson put up a more substantial building there, a one-and-a-half-story adobe. (if you go to 827 Grant Avenue today you will find a Chinese souvenir shop selling postcards, touristy T-shirts, and black-and-white striped Alcatraz Penitentiary hats at the site of the old "Casa Grande.")

Jacob P. Leese became Yerba Buena's second home-owner when he built his house next door to Richardson. Leese followed his neighbor's example by taking Mexican citizenship and marrying into a prominent family: Rosa Vallejo, **General Mariano Vallejo**'s sister, became Leese's wife. On April 15, 1838, Rosa gave birth to Rosalia Leese, Yerba Buena's first baby.

Jacob P. Leese

The Leese Family

Jacob Leese's former partner, **Nathan Spear**, remained in business in Yerba Buena, where he was joined by his 16-year-old nephew, **William Heath Davis**. Both were experienced merchants, having spent some years trading with Kanaka natives from the Sandwich Islands (as Hawaii was then called). Davis, in fact, had been born in Hawaii and was known as "Kanaka Bill." The two expanded their business inventory to include rum, which proved to be a very popular item. The gallon that cost one dollar in Hawaii fetched three or four dollars in Yerba Buena, and the enterprise prospered. By the early 1840s, Spear had the finest house and store in town; two ships working the trade route to the Sandwich Islands; and a successful flour mill, powered by a team of six mules. When Spear died suddenly of heart disease at age forty-seven, all Yerba Buena mourned his passing, and ships in the harbor flew their flags at half mast. His name was later given to one of the new streets south of Market as the Cove was filled in.

In 1841, the Hudson's Bay Company constructed a building next door to where Leese and Spear had conducted business. The British had been major players in West Coast trading for many years, dating back to George Vancouver's 1792 visit to San Francisco Bay. (Indeed, American traders like Leese and Spear complained that the initials HBC, of Hudson's Bay Company, actually stood for "Here Before Christ".) But the Hudson's Bay Company closed its Yerba Buena store in 1845, following a scandal: the manager, William Glen Rae, was caught in an adulterous affair and became the town's first suicide. The building, which stood at the corner of Clay and Montgomery, was sold to an American, **William D. M. Howard**.

William D. M. Howard
San Francisco's 1st philanthropist

The purchase turned out to be Howard's big break. He had come to Yerba Buena years earlier as an agent for a firm from his native Boston, buying California's only real exports, hides and tallow. Howard soon left the firm and went into business with a partner, Henry Mellus. After they bought the HBC building and branched out into dry goods, the business did well. Later they were positioned to cash in on the phenomenal growth of San Francisco during the Gold Rush.

Howard became a wealthy pillar of the community, active in civic affairs, and San Francisco's first philanthropist. He headed Yerba Buena's rag-tag militia of twenty or thirty men during the Mexican War, served on the first American town council, and helped oversee construction of the first city-financed wharf, the Broadway pier. Howard also paid to have one of San Francisco's first fire engines brought around the Horn from New York, and at one point personally paid teachers' salaries when the City couldn't afford to.

Howard and Mellus both had streets named for them in San Francisco, running next to each other (as befitted partners) a couple of blocks south of Market Street. Later, when Howard bought out his partner's share of the business, Mellus angrily charged that he had been cheated. Howard retaliated by using his influence on the town council to have the name of Mellus Street changed to Natoma Street (the name of an Indian tribe on the Feather River). Today, Howard is immortalized in a major thoroughfare, but who has ever heard of Henry Mellus?

Yerba Buena in the mid-1830s was a sleepy place. New arrivals to the town simply camped wherever they pleased, and an *ad hoc* system of pathways criss-crossed the town, connecting the Presidio, the Mission, and the Cove. By **Francisco de Haro**'s second term (1838-1839), Yerba Buena had grown to the point where Richardson's original rough sketch of the town was inadequate, and a true survey was needed.

De Haro hired a young Swiss seaman, Jean Jaques Vioget, to lay out some streets for the town. Eight blocks were plotted, bounded by present-day Montgomery, Grant, Pacific, and Sacramento. Each block was divided into six lots, fifty *varas* square. (The *vara*, or "Spanish yard," was a measure about thirty-three inches long.) In one of the blocks, four lots were reserved as a public plaza; this plaza is now the site of Portsmouth Square.

The first street, which ran in front of Leese's and Richardson's lots, came to be called "*Calle de la Fundación*" (Street of the Founding), though later its name was changed, first to DuPont Street, and then to Grant Avenue. The other streets in the Vioget survey were simply marked off with crude fencing and left nameless. The layout was somewhat vague. In 1843, the boundaries of Richardson's lot had to be shifted a little so that it would abut more squarely on *Calle de la Fundación*, but no one seemed to mind.

Vioget, who had come to Yerba Buena as master of his own ship, was apparently a likable and talented man. He ran one of the first taverns in town, complete with a billiard table, and he did a commendable job of Yerba Buena's first survey. But he made the streets very narrow. Kearny Street was only a little over forty-five feet wide; *Calle de la Fundación* was forty-four feet. Both streets subsequently had to be widened, Kearny to seventy-five feet wide (but only from Market to Broadway) and *Calle de la Fundación* to seventy-four feet (but only from Market to Bush). As you walk through Chinatown, notice that the old *Calle de la Fundación*, now Grant Avenue, remains at its original width of forty-four feet everywhere north of Bush Street, which creates traffic and public safety nightmares. (Try to picture yourself driving a fire engine down Grant past the rows of parked cars!)

In 1845 the Vioget survey was expanded to include Broadway and Vallejo on the north, California, Pine, and Bush on the south, and Stockton and Powell on the east. Street widths varied, since it wasn't until later that a standard of sixty eight-feet-and-nine-inches was settled on for the Fifty Vara survey (i.e. - to the north of Market Street and into the Western Addition). In the Hundred Vara survey (south of Market and into the Mission District) the standard street width was eighty-two feet-six inches, but again with a number of exceptions.

Sound confusing? It was. Still, the haphazard approach to determining street width was nothing compared to the casual treatment accorded the map itself. Vioget's plan was kept behind the bar of Robert Ridley's tavern on Kearny Street and had the names of Yerba Buena's landowners written on each lot. When lots were resold or when new lots were added, erasures and corrections were made directly on the map.

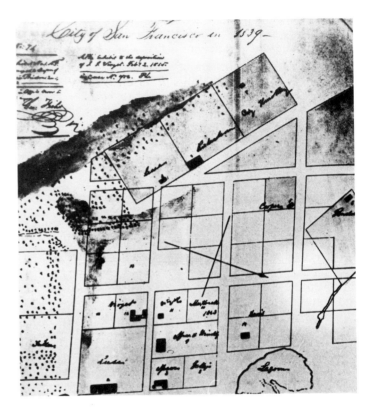

The 1839 Vioget map.

John Henry Brown, the innkeeper of the earliest Yerba Buena hotel, Portsmouth House, wrote in his *Reminiscences* (1882):

> *The map got so much soiled and torn from the rough usage it received that Captain Hinckley volunteered to make a new one. He tried several times, but being very nervous he could not succeed in making the lines straight, so he got me to do the work, according to his instructions. The original maps were left in the barroom until after the raising of the American Flag [in Portsmouth Square, July 1846].*

The 1830s and early 1840s were care-free times in the Bay Area. A few dozen families ran the show. Some, like Moraga, Vallejo, and Martínez, controlled vast tracts of land in the inland ranches, and were to have towns named after them. Others, like **José de Jesús Noé**, **Francisco Guerrero**, and Francisco de Haro, owned large ranches on San Francisco peninsula, and enjoyed terms as alcalde in Yerba Buena.

But the Mexicans never achieved secure possession of Alta California. Their population was never large enough, nor industrious enough, to exercise true control over the area. The inefficient Mexican bureaucracy, the lack of markets for agricultural products, and the comfortable indolence caused by the availability of free Indian labor all conspired to limit Mexican development of the spectacularly promising land.

Other nations cast a greedy eye on California. The British in particular sought to extend their influence south from the Oregon territory (which included present-day British Columbia) by trade if possible, or perhaps by other means if necessary.

Ultimately, the fate of California depended on forces far beyond its own borders, and in particular, of course, on the Americans.

Chapter 3

The Americans

By the mid-1840s, word of California's vast potential was starting to find its way to the outside world via merchants, trappers, and whalers. Richard Henry Dana's popular novel, *Two Years Before the Mast*, published in 1840, was based on his voyage to San Francisco Bay on a hide-and-tallow trader from Boston. Dana made a prediction as he sailed out of the Bay a couple of days after Christmas, 1835: "If California ever becomes a prosperous country, this bay will be the center of its prosperity."

John C. Fremont published a "Report of the Exploring Expedition to Oregon and Northern California," in 1845, recounting his exploits with Kit Carson in 1842-1844, a journey which brought Fremont fame as "The Pathfinder." The report was eagerly read, especially for its description of the route West, and ran through four printings.

At that time American expansionist fever was high: 1845 was the year that Texas was annexed, as well as the year that the expression, "Manifest Destiny" was coined to justify American ownership of the continent from sea to shining sea. Long before the Gold Rush, American immi-

John C. Fremont
"The Pathfinder"

gration caused the last Mexican governor of Alta California, **Pio Pico**, to lament: "We find ourselves threatened by hordes of Yankee emigrants . . . whose progress we cannot arrest."

American intentions were hardly a secret. Back in 1835 President Jackson had offered the Mexican government $500,000 for the San Francisco peninsula and lands to the north, but the offer was rejected. More ominously, in 1842 the U.S. Navy's Pacific Commander, Thomas Ap Catesby Jones, attacked Monterey, mistakenly thinking that war had broken out. Following his standing orders to the letter (albeit prematurely), he forced the Mexicans to surrender the fort and ran the Stars and Stripes up the flagpole. When he learned of his mistake the next day, he ran them right back down again, apologized profusely, and made a red-faced departure.

Fremont certainly made no secret of his enthusiasm for California. It was he who christened the entrance to the Bay, "Chrysopylae", the Golden Gate. And, he believed that the earthly paradise within the Gate should rightly belong to America.

Fremont had married Jessie Benton, daughter of Senator Thomas Hart Benton of Missouri, a fervent expansionist whose impassioned speeches to Congress had earned him the nickname, "The Thunderer." The apple doesn't fall far from the tree: daughter Jessie was a prolific author, banging the drum for Manifest Destiny in numerous best-selling books. (John C. Fremont himself wrote very little; writing gave him nosebleeds.)

In the spring of 1845, **President Polk** sent Fremont to California with the U.S. Topographical Corps, ostensibly to find the best overland routes. The Mexicans were wary, and rightly so. When they ordered Fremont to leave, he instead began fortifying a hilltop position to do battle. Then, calculating the odds against his sixty-two men, he withdrew towards Oregon amidst a covering salvo of bluster and rant. He would be back.

Pressure was building for U.S. control of California, especially since the British were making distinctly proprietary noises themselves. President Polk sent a secret message to his U.S. Consul in Monterey, **Thomas O. Larkin,** urging him to "exert the greatest vigilance in discovering and defeating any attempt which may be made by foreign governments to acquire a control over [California]."

Larkin appreciated the difficulty of Polk's position. He couldn't simply send in troops, for the U.S. and Mexico weren't at war; but he couldn't stand by and do nothing or the prize might well be lost. The ideal situation would be for California to be led somehow to seek annexation voluntarily, and then, wrote Polk, "if the people should desire to unite their destiny with ours, they would be received as brethren."

Larkin had many qualities that made him a good candidate for secret agent, of the diplomatic, not the cloak-and-dagger variety. Larkin, unlike many early American settlers, had kept his U.S. citizenship, living in Monterey under a visa arrangement called a "*carta de seguridad.*" In his hide-and-tallow business he was known as an honest trader, and was trusted and well-liked by the local Mexicans.

Thomas O. Larkin
Businessman and Secret Agent

He had even acted as translator and negotiator in the Commodore Jones fiasco. The good relations he developed with the Mexican population (the "Californios") were to pay off handsomely later; in fact, they probably saved Larkin's life. He was captured by the Californios during the war and kept prisoner for several months in Santa Barbara and Los Angeles, but he was never mistreated and was later released unharmed.

He had come to California from New England with the stated plan of becoming wealthy, either in business or, if necessary, by marriage. As things turned out, Larkin married Mrs. Rachel Hobson Holmes, a widow of only average financial means who had shared the long voyage from Boston with him. But Larkin's hide-and-tallow business, which he expanded to include lumber, food, and liquor, more than satisfied his dreams of financial success. Like William Richardson in Yerba Buena, Larkin in Monterey became a prosperous and respected businessman.

After the war Larkin played a key role in the California Constitutional Convention, where his tact and diplomacy were much admired. In the San Francisco survey conducted in 1849 by **William M. Eddy,** the westernmost street running north-to-south was named for Thomas O. Larkin. Everything west of this line in later surveys became known as the Western Addition, though the generally accepted definition changed over the years (many old-timers will tell you that the Western Addition starts at Van Ness Avenue). New district names like "the Richmond" and "Sunset" were later added.

Larkin's vice-consul is remembered in a narrow street that runs the three blocks from Clay to Pine, between Montgomery and Sansome. A brass plaque on the back of 343 Sansome Street carries a bust and inscription:

William Alexander Leidesdorff
1810-1848
Builder • Entrepreneur • Visionary
Pioneer • San Franciscan • African-American

It's difficult to imagine, standing in this quiet alley today, that it was once part of the bustling heart of downtown San Francisco. The What Cheer House, opened by R. B. Woodward, on the corner of Sacramento Street in 1852, was a busy hotel. It later housed the City's first free library and first museum. Out in front, horse-drawn cabs crowded Leidesdorff Street, and tinsmiths and vendors bellowed their sales pitches. Housewives bought and sold penny stocks in an informal open-air stock exchange. (The stockbrokers in the official exchange just around the corner derisively called them "mudhens.") Their dreams of instant riches were shared by other women in the street, who conducted business of a somewhat less savory nature. And all manner of goods were hauled up from the piers, past the saloons and gambling houses, and into town.

William Leidesdorff was born in the West Indies, on the island of St. Thomas, the son of a Danish seaman and a native woman. At an early age he was adopted by an English planter, who saw to the boy's education. Later the Englishman sent Leidesdorff to live with his brother in New

Brass plaque at 343 Sansome Street of William Alexander Leidesdorff

Orleans, where he grew up in the ways of a Southern gentleman. When his benefactor died, Leidesdorff inherited the considerable estate.

The fairy tale continued. He fell in love with a beautiful, young woman named Hortense, whose family proudly traced their roots back to Louis XIV of France. But the young prince and princess were not to live happily ever after. On the eve of their wedding, William revealed to Hortense the secret of his mulatto birth, and her parents called the marriage off. Leidesdorff sold his possessions, bought a large schooner, and resolved to start a new life in California. Hortense, it is said, died of a broken heart on the day he set sail.

William Leidesdorff arrived in Yerba Buena in 1841 and fell terminally ill with a brain fever just seven years later. In those seven years he achieved many notable "firsts": he established the first steamship run between Yerba Buena and Sacramento; he was a member of the first American town council; and he was on the commission to build the town's first public school. When he died he was buried in a place of honor, within the walls of Mission Dolores.

The story does not end here, however. Leidesdorff left no will. There were numerous claimants to the estate, nearly all of them obvious frauds, but one group had what appeared at the time to be a solid claim. These were the descendants of a certain Hungarian, Wolf Leidesdorfer, who were living in the West Indies.

At this point **Captain Joseph L. Folsom** entered the picture. A New Hampshire native, Folsom had been a cadet, and later a teacher, at West Point. He had come to California with the Stevenson Regiment, a group of volunteers from New York who had arrived too late to actually fight in the war, but who nevertheless played an important role in keeping the peace afterwards. He had already shown himself to be a shrewd real estate speculator, investing every cent he could spare to buy up properties in the sandy hills of Yerba Buena.

Like everyone else in town, Folsom knew of the Leidesdorff estate. When Leidesdorff died in May 1848, the forty-one City lots he owned were worth little. At that time a 50-vara lot in the main part of town could be had for just under $16. A 100-vara lot south of Market Street cost less than $30. But with the Gold Rush, Leidesdorff's estate had soared in value, and Folsom was determined to have it.

He sailed to the West Indies and bullied the legitimate claimants into selling him their rights for a proverbial song. When Folsom arrived back in San Francisco he had with him all the legal papers he needed to claim the bulk of Leidesdorff's fortune. Folsom was able to parlay his winnings into large parcels of real estate in San Francisco, as well as 35,500 acres of land northeast of Sacramento. All these holdings continued to increase in value exponentially as San Francisco and California grew. The *Annals of San Francisco*, written shortly before Folsom's death in 1855, called him "one of the wealthiest citizens of California." Both Folsom Street and the city of Folsom (on the site of the inherited lands) commemorate the former West Pointer.

A year after his embarrassing retreat towards Oregon, John C. Fremont was back with grand ideas in mind for wresting California from Mexican hands:

First, select a dozen men who have nothing to lose but everything to gain;
second, encourage them to commit depredations against **General Castro**; . . .
third make prisoners of some of the principal men, and thus provoke Castro to strike the first blow in a war with the United States.

This prescription bears remarkable similarities to the Bear Flag Revolt that occurred later that same year. The actual extent of Fremont's involvement in the revolt is still debated. Americans in the Sacramento Valley had harbored grievances for years against Mexican policies, and they eventually may have acted without Fremont's incitement. But Fremont certainly did nothing to discourage false rumors that two-hundred-and-fifty armed Californios were headed their way, burning homes and destroying crops and livestock. And when a group of Americans under **Ezekiel Merritt** seized a herd of Mexican horses being moved from Sonoma to the Santa Clara Valley, Fremont's active encouragement no doubt led to the next major step in the revolt, the arrest of Don Mariano Guadalupe Vallejo.

Don Mariano Guadalupe Vallejo

Vallejo was mystified to see about thirty armed men, led by William B. Ide and Robert Semple, at the door of his Sonoma ranch at dawn on Sunday, June 14. He had no ill will for the Americans, and in fact seems to have favored California's independence from Mexico. But the presence of all these excited Yankees at that hour of the morning was puzzling, to say the least. An interpreter was at last able to translate the Americans' intentions, and Vallejo politely invited them in.

Over generous servings of Don Mariano's wine and *aguardiente*, the independence of the California Republic was declared, and a three-foot, by five-foot, flag was in-expertly stitched together. In one corner was a five-pointed star painted with red ink, and a grizzly bear (famous for not backing down) was crudely represented in the field. At the bottom of the flag were the words "California Republic" on a strip of red felt.

California's state flag is modeled on the original Bear Flag.

Mariano Vallejo, his brother Salvador, and his brother-in-law Jacob Leese, were all taken prisoner and held at Sutter's Fort. At this point, Fremont formally joined the Bear Flaggers and sent a letter to his father-in-law, Senator Benton, resigning his commission in the U.S. Army. This action would, if necessary, allow the U.S. Government to deny any connection with the Bear Flag Revolt. On July 2, Fremont, Semple and company marched on San Francisco and, finding that Alcalde William Hinckley died the day before, arrested Port Captain (and saloon owner) Robert Ridley instead.

The whole Bear Flag episode might be recalled as a comic opera but for the fact that several Californios had been killed. A small band of Fremont's men, including Kit Carson, had chanced upon the twin sons of Francisco de Haro and an old man (Ramon Berryessa, the father of Sonoma's alcalde) and killed them. The three were unarmed. Carson defended his actions, saying that Fremont had told him, with a dismissive wave of the hand, "I have no room for prisoners."

There's no telling how far the Bear Flag Revolt would have gone; perhaps Fremont would have become the Sam Houston of an independent country called the California Republic. But war, real war, had already erupted between Mexican and American forces near the Rio Grande, in Texas, more than a month earlier, and the revolt was rendered irrelevant by the larger historical picture.

California's problems had not been directly responsible for the start of the war, but control of California quickly became one of the war's objectives. Commodore **John D. Sloat**, commanding the U.S. Pacific Fleet, had moved his forces north from the waters off Mazatlán, Mexico. On July 2, the day the Bear Flaggers arrived in San Francisco, he was anchored in Monterey Bay. Sloat was not known for decisive action, and it wasn't until five days later, after conferring with Thomas Larkin and drawing up plans and proclamations, that he came ashore with two-hundred-and-fifty men to take possession of the unoccupied Monterey Presidio.

A similar scene was enacted in Yerba Buena on July 9. **Captain John B. Montgomery**, on the *Portsmouth*, anchored in the Cove and landed with seventy men near Clark's Point unopposed. A Petty Officer from the *Portsmouth*'s crew, Joseph Downey, later wrote a number of articles for the *Golden Era*, a San Francisco weekly in the 1850s. His reminiscences were published under the title "Filings from an Old Saw," and provide an interesting first-hand account of the American "capture" of Yerba Buena:

> *And to the soul-inspiring air of Yankee Doodle from our band, consisting of one drum and fife, with an occasional put-in from a stray dog or disconsolate jackass in the line of march, [we] trudged proudly up through Montgomery Street to Clay, up Clay to the Plaza . . . and in a moment, amid a roar of cannon from the ship, and hurrahs of the ship's company, the viva's of the Californians, the cheers of the Dutchmen, and barking of dogs, braying of jackasses, and a general confusion of sounds from every living thing within hearing, that flag floated proudly up . . .*

Montgomery had written a proclamation suitable to the occasion, which was read by one of his officers and listened to with a mixture of boredom and impatience. Then everyone was at last able to proceed with the important business of getting a drink:

> The Indians consequently rushed frantically to one pulperee, Captain Leidesdorff and the aristocracy to Bob Ridley's barroom, and the second class and the Dutch to Tinker's. The houses being on three of the four corners of the square, one [standing] in the barracks could see the maneuvers of each of them. For the first hour things went quiet enough, but soon the strong water began to work, and such a confusion of sounds could never have been heard since the Babel Tower . . . This Pandemonium lasted for some hours, in fact until sundown, when the Commandante sent a guard to warn the revelers that as the town was now under martial law, they must cease their orgies and return to their respective homes. But few, however, were able to do so, and the greater part of them either slept in Tinker's alley or on the grass in the Plaza.

When the festivities ended, Yerba Buena's two-hundred or so residents turned their attention to defending against

Captain John B. Montgomery

Washington Bartlett
Yerba Buena's first American alcalde

the expected Mexican counterattack. Civic-minded William Howard was put in charge of a small volunteer militia. Lookouts were posted on top of Telegraph Hill (then called simply, "*Loma Alta*", the "High Hill") to watch for Mexican or British ships. Dirt was mounded up for a gun emplacement on the north shore of the Cove near Clark's Point. (This was the battery that later gave Battery Street its name.) And **Robert F. Stockton**, who had taken over Sloat's command of the Pacific Squadron at the end of July, enrolled the Bear Flaggers into the U.S. Army as volunteers.

None of these preparations proved necessary; for Yerba Buena the war was already over. The dusty little settlement was passing into American hands just as it was becoming a true town. The last Mexican alcalde, **José de Jesús Noé**, had been the first to reside and hold office "in town" instead of out at the Mission. The cluster of tents and simple buildings along the Cove was taking on a sense of permanence and the almost palpable air of a place with a great future.

Montgomery appointed one of his lieutenants, **Washington A. Bartlett**, to be Yerba Buena's first American alcalde. Bartlett's appointment was confirmed in an election held the following month, in which he ran against Bob Ridley. Before his term of office expired in February 1847, Bartlett made a couple of rulings that had lasting effects on the town. First, he ordered the name "Yerba Buena" changed to "San Francisco," on January 30, 1847. Second, and more importantly, he ordered a new survey of San Francisco, and hired an Irishman, **Jasper O'Farrell,** to carry out the task.

Unlike Vioget before him, O'Farrell was a bona fide civil engineer and a capable surveyor. He had worked for the Mexicans, determining the boundaries of land grants throughout the Bay Area. In this capacity he had witnessed the de Haro/Berryessa killings, which he protested vigorously. His public attack on Fremont concluded:

> *I must say that I feel degraded in soiling paper with the name of a man, whom for that act, I must always look upon with contempt and consider as a murderer and coward . . .*

Some say that the public shame over this incident clouded Fremont's otherwise heroic reputation and was responsible for his loss in the 1856 Presidential elections, in which he ran as the new Republican party's first candidate. Even the catchy campaign slogan, "Free Soil, Free Land, Free Men, and Fremont," was not enough to prevent victory by James Buchanan.

In San Francisco, O'Farrell's first difficulty was to correct the Vioget survey, which was two-and-a-half degrees out of square. Several property lines and street boundaries had to be swung slightly to one side to effect the change, which property owners angrily dubbed "the O'Farrell Twist."

O'Farrell avoided Vioget's other mistake, too-narrow streets, by insisting on street widths of at least 75-80 feet. A larger problem was to accomodate San Francisco's hilly terrain. One ideas was to have the streets curve to conform to the steepness of the hills, but would-be real estate specu-

Typical sidewalk on a steep City street. This one is on Kearny Street, north of Broadway.

32

lators objected, reasoning that a rectangular grid would be easier (and more profitable) to sub-divide later. As a result, some of San Francisco's streets have to climb and descend at absurdly steep angles. Filbert Street between Hyde and Leavenworth, for example, is thirty-one-and-a-half degrees. Visitors to the City are always astonished to see sidewalks built in the form of stairways on the steeper streets.

The one exception O'Farrell made to the regular rectangular street pattern was Market Street, which ran from the Cove towards the Mission at a fifty-four degree angle to the grid. Even this decision might have been forgiven by San Francisco's property owners, but O'Farrell also made Market Street "too wide", some one hundred-and-twenty feet. The extra width was attained at the expense of the adjacent lots, and the owners of those lots were absolutely furious. O'Farrell wisely left town, taking a boat to Sausalito, and from there hopping a fast horse to Sonoma. Eventually the public furor died down. Indeed, some years later the City had cause to be grateful for the "too wide" Market Street, since it made it possible to build street car tracks down the middle of the street and still leave room for vehicle traffic on either side.

O'Farrell's survey extended the streets already laid out by Vioget and added about eight hundred acres to the town. To the north, O'Farrell plotted streets as far as Francisco Street, which was where the Bay waters then met land. Leavenworth Street marked the western edge of the survey, and Post Street the south.

One curious feature of O'Farrell's survey is that it projected streets eastward into the shallows and mud flats of Yerba Buena Cove. Early San Francisco was virtually without public funds, apart from the occasional fine collected for drunkenness. The hope was that the City could profit from the sale of these "water lots"; further-more, moving the shoreline out to deeper water with a little bit of judicious landfilling would make it possible to construct better wharves and docking facilities. It was thought at the time that a block or two of eastward expansion would meet the City's needs for at least twenty years.

The only problem was that the City did not own any land below the high tide line. **Edwin Bryant**, who had succeeded Washington Bartlett as alcalde in February 1847, petitioned California's military governor for legal right to the water lots. In March the proclamation was issued:

I do hereby grant, convey, and release to the town of San Francisco . . . the beach and water lots on the east front of said town . . . provided the said ground hereby ceded shall be divided into lots and sold by public auction to the highest bidder . .

In three days of brisk bidding in July, about four-hundred-and-fifty water lots were snapped up at prices of $50 to $100 each. When the tide was high, the proud owners could row out and paddle around their "property."

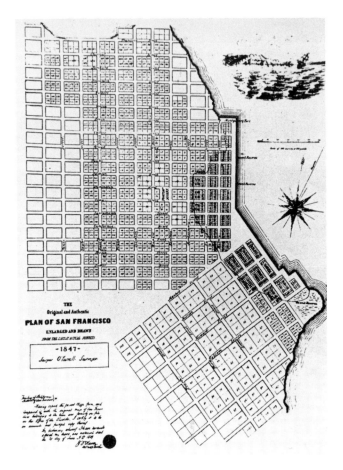

1847 O'Farrell Map of San Francisco

Portion of 1849 William Eddy Map of San Francisco

View of San Francisco, formerly Yerba Buena , in March 1847, before the discovery of gold. The large ship to the left is the merchant ship, Vandalia, *and the large ship in the center is the U.S.S.* Portsmouth.

The projections that it would take twenty years to fill in the water lots turned out to be wildly inaccurate. The Gold Rush brought so many ships to San Francisco (six-hundred-and-twenty-six vessels were in the Bay, in July 1850) that the Cove was soon choked with hundreds of square-riggers.

Some of the ships were hauled up onto shore and used for warehouses, shops, and even homes, but the great majority remained at anchor, where the gold-hungry crews had abandoned them. The ships very quickly rotted right where they were, to be buried later under vast quantities of sand taken from San Francisco's hills. Seven years after the auction, not just one or two blocks but all of Yerba Buena Cove was dry land, and a $100 water lot was worth $15,000.

As you stand outside the Transamerica Pyramid at Columbus and Montgomery, consider this: you are at the edge of the old Cove. If you continue south on Montgomery, following the old shoreline for a block-and-a-half to Commercial Street, you will be at the site of Jacob Leese's building "on the beach." Everything east of you, including most of San Francisco's Financial District, sits on landfill. In fact, modern excavations for skyscrapers have occasionally uncovered remains of ships that carried 49ers around the Horn.

The military governor who ceded the water lost to San Francisco was Major General Stephen Watts Kearny. He had been a military man since the War of 1812, in which he served as an eighteen-year-old lieutenant. His rise through the ranks over the next thirty years led to this appointment as commander of Fort Leavenworth, Kansas in 1846. When

Old Saint Mary's Church, a Chinese pagoda and the Transamerica Pyramid share a City skyline.

General Pio Pico

hostilities with Mexico began that year, he assembled a force of nearly 1600 men, the "Army of the West," and marched to Santa Fe, New Mexico. The Mexican forces there retreated in the face of Kearny's overwhelming numbers, and the town was taken with no real opposition. At the end of September, Kearny and a small contingent of his forces set out for California.

By that time General Stockton's troops, who now included the former Bear Flaggers and recently re-commissioned Major John C. Fremont, had sailed south from Yerba Buena on the *Cyane*. Stockton and three-hundred-and-sixty men landed at San Pedro, near Los Angeles, and marched toward the city; Fremont's group would disembark at San Diego and go north to meet them there.

Militarily, the situation had all the makings of a disaster. Mexican generals Pio Pico and José Castro (a direct descendant of one of Anza's soldiers, Isidro de Castro) had massed some 2,000 troops in the area, with considerable artillery. Stockton had but one mortar, and his men were mostly sailors from the *Cyane*, inexperienced at combat on land.

Stockton conceived an ingenious plan. He had his men march along a ridge in full view of the opposing army. When the first men reached the end of the ridge they ducked down out of sight and doubled back to the start of the line. What the Mexicans saw was a seemingly endless column of American soldiers marching along the ridge. The bluff worked. Castro and Pico fled south, and Stockton was able to enter Los Angeles unopposed. Unfortunately, he left only fifty men to occupy the town while he returned to Yerba Buena, and within a few months Los Angeles was back under Mexican control. It would have to be retaken by the Americans at the end of the year.

Kearny, meanwhile, had arrived in California and had run into trouble almost immediately. On December 6, near an Indian village known as San Pascual, the war's bloodiest battle was fought. The American forces were exhausted by the march from Santa Fe and were no match for the skilled mounted lancers under General Pico. Two quick attacks left eighteen Americans dead and twenty seriously wounded, including General Kearny himself.

When night fell, Lieutenant **Edward F. Beale** and Kit Carson managed to sneak through the Mexican lines and get help from Stockton in San Diego. The one-hundred-and-eighty reinforcements allowed Kearny's troops to extricate themselves from San Pascual and join forces with Stockton.

It was then that Kearny and Stockton faced one of the bitterest clashes of the war, with each other. It is probably a truism of military history that whenever an army general and a navy commodore have had to work together they have argued first over who would be in charge. Kearny and Stockton were no exception. As a compromise, Stockton was placed nominally in command, and Kearny was put in charge of operations. That settled, they proceeded with the last military action of the war in California, the retaking of Los Angeles.

General Robert F. Stockton

The battle itself was anticlimactic. The Californios seemed to realize that further resistance was pointless, and withdrew after token, long-range artillery fire and a few half-hearted cavalry charges. On January 10, Kearny and Stockton marched into the plaza in Los Angeles.

Fremont and his four-hundred men arrived from the San Fernando valley two days later, and the intra-American rivalry ignited all over again. He recognized Stockton, not Kearny, as the officer in command. Even worse, Fremont himself negotiated the treaty of surrender, acting as what he called "military commander," without higher authorization.

The terms of surrender, the "Cahuenga Capitulation," were generous and conciliatory, and ended the fighting in California with none of the bitterness that usually accompanies military conquest. Kearny's terms for Fremont, however, were far less forgiving. He dragged "the Pathfinder" back to Fort Leavenworth, placed him under arrest, and shipped him off to Washington, D.C. for court martial. Found guilty, then pardoned by President Polk, Fremont resigned his commission anyway and left the service. A dozen years later, Fremont would have the last laugh: when the Civil War broke out, the Union Army asked him to come back, gave him the rank of Major General, and put him in charge of the entire Western Department.

For his part, Stockton returned to newly-named San Francisco as a conquering hero. Not only had he brilliantly vanquished an enemy of superior numbers, he had wisely treated that enemy with good will and compassion. Prisoners had been released simply on their promise not to fight again, no atrocities had been committed, and the transition to American rule in California had been accomplished without major bloodshed. The *Annals of San Francisco* recorded that when Stockton came to the city

> *the entire population of that place and the adjacent country gave him a formal reception—men, women, and children marching to the low-water mark to meet him—and addressing him in terms of the most exalted praise and ardent devotion.*

The war gave San Francisco a new honor role of heroes; by happy coincidence, Jasper O'Farrell's survey had given the City new streets in need of names. It was only natural that the former should be applied to the latter. The name of Calle de la Fundación was discarded as non-American. It was renamed "DuPont Street," in honor of **Samuel F. DuPont,** who had commanded Stockton's flag-ship *Congress*. (Although the name of DuPont Street was later changed to "Grant Avenue," many Cantonese-speaking residents of Chinatown today still call the street "DuPont Gai.")

Kearny and Stockton were assigned the major streets on either side of DuPont, and Captain Montgomery's name was given to the only remaining street between town and the water. As the Cove was filled in, making First Street not the "first street" at all, the names of John C. Fremont and Edward F. Beale were used for two of the new streets south of Market.

On February 2, 1848, the Treaty of Guadalupe Hidalgo ended the Mexican-American War, but this historic event was to have little direct effect on San Francisco. Fighting in California had already ended more than a year earlier with the Cahuenga Capitulation, and in San Francisco the entire war had passed without a shot being fired in anger. The event that was to change the City's history forever had already occurred nine days before Guadalupe Hidalgo, yet for a long time it went virtually unnoticed.

Chapter 4

Gold

On July 31, 1846, the 450-ton *Brooklyn* sailed into San Francisco Bay, after a five-month voyage around the Horn from New York, with a stop in the Sandwich Islands. On board were seventy men, sixty-eight women, and nearly one-hundred children, all Mormons searching for a new land in which to practice their religion free from persecution. Their leader, **Sam Brannan**, stood on the *Brooklyn*'s deck in Yerba Buena Cove and felt his heart sink at the sight before him: the American flag was flying from Portsmouth Square, where John B. Montgomery had raised it just three weeks before.

"That damn rag again!" cursed Brannan. California had been claimed by the United States, and the free exercise of Mormon tenets, especially polygamy, would be illegal.

Equally disappointing, Brigham Young and his overland party of Mormons, who had planned to meet Brannan's group in California, were nowhere to be seen. They had made it only as far as the Great Salt Lake, where Young had decided to establish the new Zion. Brannan, of course, knew nothing of this. What he did know was that Yerba Buena,

Sam Brannan

windy, damp, and virtually devoid of vegetation on its sandy, fog-swept hills, was not the paradise he had hoped for. But at least the Saints of Nauvoo had arrived well-prepared. The *Brooklyn's* hold contained extensive stores of colonizing supplies: tools, farming implements, construction materials, seeds, even a printing press. They would try to make the best of it.

When the Mormons came ashore, they effectively doubled the population of Yerba Buena. According to Joseph Downey, one of Montgomery's men who wrote a series of articles in the 1850's under the pseudonym, "The Old Saw," the group camped in an empty lot bounded by Kearny, Montgomery, Clay, and Washington, on the eastern side of Portsmouth Square. (A great many visitors have "camped" on this spot since then: it is now the site of the Holiday Inn.)

Sam Brannan was not what one might picture as the stereotypical Mormon Elder. Barrel-chested, loud, supremely confident, and a tireless self-promoter, the twenty-six-year-old Brannan quickly carved a prominent place for himself in Yerba Buena. Early along on the road to riches Brannan collided with the Mormon leadership in Salt Lake, who claimed he had absconded with church tithes. He had. In the first case brought to trial in an American court in Yerba Buena, a defiant Brannan escaped conviction, and later said he would return the funds "when Brigham Young sends me a receipt signed by the Lord." No such receipt was forthcoming, and neither were the funds.

Brannan, now an ex-Mormon Elder, became a civic leader and force to be reckoned with. Using the printing press brought on the *Brooklyn*, he published the *California Star*, a four-page weekly whose first issue appeared on January 9, 1847. That first issue promised that "all private pique, personal feeling and jealousy will be laid aside" in the interests of professional reporting, but publication of the *Star* was not always a happy affair. **Elbert P. Jones**, the paper's first editor, was succeeded by Edward Kemble after Kemble won a fist fight with Jones and physically threw him out of the office. (The *Star* reported only that Jones had "withdrawn" as editor.)

Sam Brannan was not above using the *Star* as his personal soapbox to make his viewpoints known to the other citizens of Yerba Buena. A case in point was the matter of the town's name. Alcalde Washington Bartlett had ordered that "Yerba Buena" be changed to "San Francisco," on January 30, 1847. Brannan preferred "Yerba Buena" and continued to use the old name in the *Star*'s dateline for several months before finally accepting the change.

All in all, the *Star* was a pretty good paper. The *Annals of San Francisco* called it "a neat production . . . of excellent quality." It published letters from the public on major issues of the day, ran columns in both English and Spanish, and reported on world events by gathering news from the passengers and crews of ships calling at San Francisco Bay.

The California Star.

VOL. 1.   YERBA BUENA, MARCH 13, 1847.   NO. 10

The California Star's *editor, Sam Brannan, preferred the city name, Yerba Buena, to San Francisco. He made his preference public by running the paper's original banner for months after the change—which took effect January 30, 1847.*

Brannan's *Star* had been in business a little over a year when rumors began reaching San Francisco of something going on up at **John Sutter**'s ranch and fort on the American River, near the site of present-day Sacramento. It seemed that James Marshall, a carpenter in Sutter's employ, had found a gold nugget while building a lumber mill back in January. But the stories were not exactly clear on the details, and the news, as related in the *Star*, on March 18, caused no excitement. Indeed, editor Kemble spent a week nosing around Sutter's property and reported that the whole story seemed little more than a "sham . . . got up to guzzle the gullible."

The rumors persisted. One day another Sutter employee, teamster Jacob Wittmer, paid in gold for a bottle of brandy in the general store at Sutter's Fort. The store, as it happened, was owned by Sam Brannan, who decided it was time to do a little investigative journalism of his own. He needed only a few days to get his scoop: There *was* gold on the American River—lots of it!

Brannan returned to San Francisco to break the news, but not with just another article in the *Star*. That was not the Sam Brannan style. Instead, on May 12, he marched down Montgomery Street, waving a whisky bottle full of gold dust and bellowing at the top of his considerable lungs, "Gold! Gold on the American River!"

Brannan's cry marked the pivotal moment in San Francisco history. The town, in 1848, had been an untidy collection of perhaps one-hundred-and-fifty buildings (many of them canvass tents) clustered around Yerba Buena Cove. In the next three years, it had at least 150,000 people descend upon it. True, most stayed only briefly on their way to the gold fields, but even so, San Francisco's permanent population in 1851 was almost 30,000. This made it roughly the same size as contemporary Chicago, with one startling difference: fully 85% of the population were adult males. In Mark Twain's famous observation, [there was] "Nothing juvenile, nothing feminine visible anywhere."

Paradoxically, the first effect of the Gold Rush was to render San Francisco virtually deserted. One report claims that only twelve able-bodied men remained in the entire town in the first few months after Sam Brannan's stroll down Montgomery Street. This is certainly an exaggeration, but a genuine exodus did occur. Even the already prominent and well-off were not immune to gold fever. Jacob Leese and Jasper O'Farrell, with two partners, spent three months on the Feather River and took out $75,000 worth of the metal.

Monterey, too, was nearly a ghost town. Walter Colton, the alcalde of that city, recorded poetically:

> *Husband and wife were both packing up;*
> *the blacksmith dropped his hammer,*
> *the carpenter his plane,*
> *the mason his trowel,*
> *the farmer his sickle,*
> *the baker his loaf,*
> *and the tapster his bottle.*
> *All were off to the mines.*

Colonel Richard B. Mason made the Gold Rush official in a report to the War Department on August 17, 1848. By that time, Mason, who had succeeded Kearny as Military Governor of California, was already losing the battle against desertion in the ranks. Mason's men were just as eager to get to the gold fields as the civilian population was. Although Mason tried a number of measures to stem the tide, including the granting of liberal furloughs, the soldiers who left for the gold fields rarely returned to service. One authority observed:

> *Troops are needed here, and greatly*
> *needed; but of what use is it to send them,*
> *with the positive certainty of their running*
> *off to the gold mines as soon as they*
> *arrive, taking with them whatever public*
> *property they can lay their hands on?*

Colonel Richard B. Mason

In the rest of the country, news of the gold discovery in California was met with skepticism. Even President Polk had voiced a common reaction to the reports when he called them "of such an extraordinary character as would scarcely command belief." Colonel Mason's official report claimed that there was enough gold in the Sacramento and San Joaquin River drainages to repay the Mexican-American War debt "a hundred times over." As tangible proof of the Eldorado on the western edge of the continent, a strongbox containing several thousand dollars worth of the precious metal was sent East. Seeing was believing.

Edward Beale, the lieutenant who had rescued General Kearny after the battle of San Pascual, was one of the envoys sent to Washington, D.C., with particulars of the discovery. Beale's heroics in the Mexican-American War are commemorated in Beale Street, south of Market, in what was once part of Yerba Buena Cove. Less well-known are Beale's bizarre exploits after the war. In 1852 he was made Superintendent of Indian Affairs, and in that capacity spent much time in the deserts of the American Southwest.

Sometime during his service there he was struck with a wonderful idea: what the U.S. Army really needed was a Camel Corps. Such a unit could supply the route from Fort Defiance, New Mexico, to southern California, the so-called "Wagon Road." Arguing the case for camels, Beale found support for the idea in Washington. Particularly enthusiastic was one Mississippi senator who was later to serve as Secretary of War under President Pierce. This was Jefferson Davis, future President of the Confederacy.

With the necessary funding from Congress, Beale sent a relative, David Porter, to the Middle East to buy the camels. He returned to Texas with thirty-four of them, in May 1856, and in a second trip in February of the following year he brought forty-three more. Thus seventy-seven of the beasts were landed on American soil, and the Camel Corps was born.

Camp Verde, sixty miles northwest of San Antonio, was selected as the site for training and for determining the animals' usefulness. They performed beautifully, more than living up to their reputation as the "ships of the desert." Two of the camels were ridden fully loaded in a trial run from San Bernardino to Los Angeles, and made the trip in under eight hours.

The Camel Corps' undoing was the Civil War. The military brass in Washington, preoccupied with other problems, lost interest in the project and, in 1864, had the camels auctioned in two herds. One herd remained on a Texas ranch for about a year before being driven off into the deserts of Mexico. The other herd was purchased by a Benicia, California man, and was later sold to a rancher in Sonoma. This herd died-off over time, but strange as it seems, for several years camels roamed the wine country, thanks to Edward F. Beale.

Colonel Mason's report to the War Department and Edward Beale's delegation to Washington brought the news of gold to the world and brought the world to California. Roughly one-third of the Argonauts came by ship, either around Cape Horn in a journey that could take six months from New York, or via Panama, a more expensive route that cut travel time to about ten weeks. The rest of the newcomers traveled overland, leaving from places like Independence, Missouri, and Council Bluffs, Iowa. Groups departed in the springtime after the prairie grasses had started growing, so that their animals would have pasturage. At all costs, the Sierra had to be crossed before winter storms arrived. The Donner Party had been trapped by unusually early snows in the winter of 1846-1847. Of the eighty-seven members of that group, only forty-five lived to reach California, and the suffering that drove them to cannibalism quickly became legend.

By whatever means, the route west was difficult and dangerous. A dozen ships had been lost at Cape Horn by 1853. The shortcut through the jungles of the Isthmus of Panama exposed travelers to malaria, yellow fever, and a host of other tropical afflictions. Crossing the continent by wagon train held its own dangers. Contrary to American folklore, Indian attack was not a frequent occurrence, but cholera and other diseases were epidemic. Another problem was that so many emigrants were using the established routes (fifty times as many people came in 1849 as in 1848) that animals soon overgrazed the plains along both sides of the trails. Horses and oxen died by the thousands for want of food, and the people had to walk most of the way to lighten the loads for the animals that remained. The most difficult parts of the trip came at the final stages, when exhausted emigrants were least able to cope with them. Poor planning, or simple bad luck, could spell disaster.

The overland groups' first stop in California was usually Sutter's Fort, or as Swiss-born John Sutter himself called it, "New Helvetia." Sutter had obtained two land grants from the Mexicans. The first was a 9,000 acre parcel at the junction of the American and Sacramento Rivers, including the site of present-day Sacramento. The second was Hock Farm, which straddled the Feather River farther north. In all, he controlled 50,000 acres, much of it fertile valley land, on which to build his empire. The fact that he had already mismanaged into bankruptcy his simple dry-goods store back in Bergdorff, Germany, in no way dimmed Sutter's hopes for the larger dream. Ever the optimist, Sutter incurred debt recklessly and without a backward glance. In his many letters to Thomas Larkin in Monterey, Sutter pleaded repeatedly for further extensions of credit, for yet a few more mules, a few more bags of seed, a few more tools. Surely next year's harvest would be the one that lifted his enterprise safely out of the red.

Unfortunately, that magic harvest remained elusive. One recurring problem was a lack of manpower. Sutter employed a number of Indians laborers, as well as a handful of pre-Gold Rush, American immigrants, but the workforce was never adequate to fully utilize the vast acreage at this command.

Still, from New Helvetia's modest beginnings in 1839, until its collapse a dozen years later, Sutter made remarkable progress. By 1848 his empire boasted 12,000 head of cattle, 2,000 horses and mules, 10,000 sheep, and 1,000 hogs.

John Sutter

And if Sutter was extremely foolish in assuming debt, he was also very generous in lending to others. He took the greatest pleasure in playing the role of gracious host to travelers, a kind of gatekeeper to the Promised Land. Groups coming down out of the Sierra invariably received a warm welcome at Sutter's Fort. The rescue parties that saved the survivors of the ill-fated Donner group had set out from New Helvetia, bearing supplies donated by John Sutter.

The Gold Rush should have made Sutter wealthy beyond measure, since his holdings included the best approaches to the gold fields, as well as navigable stretches of the Sacramento, Feather, and American Rivers. Sutter was simply overwhelmed by the sheer numbers of new immigrants. Wheat fields were trampled, horses and mules stolen, cattle slaughtered and eaten. In the winter of 1849-1850, one meat company in Sacramento netted $60,000 dealing exclusively in cattle stolen from John Sutter.

"My best days were just before the discovery of gold," lamented Sutter later to Congress, which he spent the last years of his life petitioning for restitution. His efforts were unsuccessful. He died in Pennsylvania on June 18, 1880, virtually penniless.

The growth of Sacramento gives a fair indication of the magnitude of the invasion that destroyed John Sutter. Robert Cleland's *History of California* (1926) reports that there were four houses in Sacramento, in April 1849. "By November its population fell but little short of 10,000."

Equally exponential growth was also occurring in San Francisco. The town quickly spread beyond the boundaries of the O'Farrell map, and in 1849, City Surveyor, William Eddy, extended the old plan. Nearly ninety blocks were added to San Francisco, pushing the western edge of the City to Larkin Street and the southern extent well into the south-of-Market area. The filling of Yerba Buena Cove continued apace, and new wharves sprouted from the eastern end of every street south of Green. Many of these wharves extended a considerable distance into the Bay. Rickety wooden plank bridges running north to south along the property lines of the water lots made it possible to walk from wharf to wharf without having to return to shore. As the Cove was filled in, the wharves became streets; the wooden pathways between wharves became the cross streets, Battery, Front, Davis, and Drumm.

Hammers and saws could be heard everywhere. The cluster of canvass tents and simple shanties that was San Francisco in 1848 was replaced by hundreds of new wood frame and brick buildings to meet the Forty-niner's residential and recreational needs: stores, hotels and lodging houses, restaurants, gambling parlors, and of course the ubiquitous saloons. An 1853 report disapprovingly counted five-hundred-thirty-seven places where liquor was sold, including forty-six gambling houses, one-hundred-and-forty-four tavern-restaurants, and forty-eight "places kept by bawds."

Gold flowed out of the hills and into San Francisco: in 1849, $10 million worth; $40 million the following year; peaking at $80 million in 1852. Virtually everything the City needed had to be imported, and commerce was king. By 1851, San Francisco ranked fourth nationally in foreign trade (right behind Boston, New York, and New Orleans). Not bad for a city whose only real export was gold.

Fortunes could be made in any number of ways. One was to corner the market in some commodity, it didn't matter which, whether it be tea or toothpicks, carpet tacks or candlewick. Buyers would meet incoming ships before they docked, offering the captain seemingly great prices for whatever the ship carried. Within a few hours the cargo could be resold on shore for an enormous profit.

Anything that miners could conceivably use soared in value. The supply of heavy blankets, high-topped boots, and camping gear couldn't keep up with the demand. The coarsest clothing sold at higher prices than the finest imported fashions. In 1850, twenty-year-old Levi Strauss came up with the idea for a pair of sturdy pants made of tent canvass, reinforced with copper rivets at the pockets and stress points. He figured it was just what miners needed while panning for gold in the rugged back-country. He was right. The Levi's empire is still growing a century-and-a-half later.

Montgomery Street became (and remains) the financial center of San Francisco. Banks opened their doors at 6 AM and didn't close them until 10 PM. Loans were made at rates of interest as high as 14% per month, which was still lower than what the gambling houses were charging. There, John Henry Brown recorded, "I have known many a gambler to pay for a loan of money as high as 10% per hour." (In compliance with the truth-in-lending laws, let the record show that the APR on such a loan is 87,600%.)

Wages and prices skyrocketed. A common laborer could demand "an ounce a day" (roughly $16) for doing the most menial tasks. Even at those unheard-of rates, laborers were hard to find. The story is told of the newly arrived passenger disembarking in San Francisco who flipped a quarter to a dock-side lay-about and ordered him to carry his suitcase up to the hotel. The scruffy-looking local threw a dollar back at him and said, "Carry it yourself." Abundant gold enabled the servant to become his own master and forced the master to be his own servant.

The upheaval caused by mass immigration also overwhelmed municipal government. In June of 1847, Military Governor Mason had instructed San Francisco's alcalde, **George Hyde**, to hold elections for a town council. Even in that pre-Gold Rush era, San Francisco had grown to the point that one man could not administer the City single-handedly. Accordingly, in September, a six-man town council was elected. Members included: William Leidesdorff; W. D. M. Howard; *Star* editor, E.P. Jones; and William Squire Clark, for whom Clark's Point is named. Clark had built Yerba Buena's first wharf on a land grant he had been given at the eastern end of Broadway. (Clark's Point and Clark's

Wharf disappeared under the landfill for the Embarcadero long ago. Future urban archaeologists searching for the remnants of the wharf and warehouse should start digging around Broadway and Battery.)

Countless tourists have ridden the cable car up from Fisherman's Wharf along the street that memorializes George Hyde, a Pennsylvania lawyer who served as clerk to Commodore Stockton. Hyde was the last San Francisco alcalde before the Gold Rush. When he built his house on the corner of Post, Market, and Montgomery, his friends all wondered why anyone would want to live "so far out of town." Within a few years Hyde would find himself in the middle of San Francisco's downtown area, his former seclusion just a memory. Today Hyde's property is occupied by three major banks, a McDonald's Restaurant, and the Montgomery Street - BART (Bay Area Rapid Transit) Station.

Hyde would also find himself in the middle of a controversy. George Hyde had a reputation for being short-tempered and hard to get along with. The Town Council, elected to assist the alcalde, spent most of its time opposing him. He was accused of altering the official City map and manipulating land sales to benefit his friends (charges that may have been true). Furthermore, there was a widespread feeling that the alcalde should be elected, not appointed by the Military Governor.

Cable Car on Hyde Street

50

In a characteristic fit of pique one day, Hyde resigned as alcalde. **John Townsend** finished out Hyde's term, from April to September 1848, and was in turn followed by a Connecticut theologian and medical doctor, named **Thaddeus Leavenworth** (alcalde from October 1848-August 1849). These two men didn't govern the City, they were overwhelmed by it. The problem, in addition to out-of-control immigration, was a chronic lack of public funds. As late as 1850, there was still no paid police force, no City jail, and no reliable system of municipal taxation. Corruption was rampant in City government, with two or even three groups competing for influence and claiming to be the legitimate Town Council during Leavenworth's term. Alcalde Leavenworth himself seems to have been honest enough, but not very decisive. One historian noted, as tactfully as possible, that "his authority was not great, and the little he had, he used sparingly."

Street maintenance was non-existent. During the winter rainy season, dirt streets became quagmires, capable of swallowing up cats, dogs, and even horses. On one street a sign warned: "This street is impassable, not even jack-assable." Sidewalks were created by dumping unwanted goods into the muck and hoping that something solid would remain on the surface. One contemporary account describes the sidewalk on the west side of Montgomery Street between Clay and Jackson:

It began with 100-pound sacks of Chilean flour. Then followed a long row of cooking stoves, over which it was necessary to carefully pick your way as some of the covers were gone. A damaged piano bridged a chasm, and beyond this a double row of tobacco boxes completed the walk.

Private companies led the way in the movement to cover streets with wooden planks. One of the first efforts was Market Street, which was planked from the center of town out to Mission Dolores in 1850. San Franciscans took advantage of this triumph of urban progress to enjoy picnics at the old Mission grounds. The company that constructed the road charged twenty-five cents for a horse and rider, and seventy-five cents for a wagon drawn by two horses.

The year 1850 saw major changes in San Francisco. The old system of an appointed alcalde was replaced by an elected mayor. A tax was levied on gambling houses to finance City projects, and a new police force and judiciary were instituted. Nationally, pressure was building for the admission of California as an American state. The discovery of gold had wrenched California and San Francisco out of their isolation, and threw them into the middle of the hottest issue of the day—slavery. The debate that was dividing the nation would have a major influence on the City for the next decade.

CHAPTER 5

Statehood

In Greek mythology, the goddess Minerva was born in a strange and fantastic way. Her father, Zeus, had a terrible headache one day. The pain got worse and worse until his head opened up and Minerva emerged, fully-formed. The designers of the California state seal placed Minerva in a central position on the emblem because she was the goddess of political wisdom, but they were also thinking of the story of her unusual birth as well. California came into being fully formed as a state without going through the customary intermediate step of becoming a territory, and there were some big headaches along the way.

That California would become a state was never really in doubt. Possession of California had been one of the war's goals from the outset, and the discovery of gold a few days before the signing of the Treaty of Guadalupe Hidalgo only made the prize that much more valuable. The first step towards statehood was to call a constitutional convention.

In September 1849, the forty-eight delegates who had been chosen from throughout California met in Monterey to begin their deliberations. California was very much in a transitional period. It was no longer Mexican, but not yet fully American either. Residents of California had been living in a legal limbo since the end of the war, unsure which laws should be enforced. Mexican law had been in effect in California since the 1820s, and there was some support for continuing with that tradition. Others said that American law should now prevail, even though California was not yet a state. It is noteworthy that nine of the convention delegates preferred Spanish to English; six of these were native-born Californios, and three were long-time residents who had married Mexican women and adopted their language and customs.

Many of the delegates were to have streets named for them in San Francisco, which is not surprising. Almost all the delegates had been in California since before the Gold Rush and had been selected for their high standing in their communities. John Sutter, whose personal empire of "New Helvetia" was about to be overrun by gold-seekers, was one of eight delegates from Sacramento. Thomas O. Larkin, a leading citizen of California since 1832, was one of Mon-

Henry Halleck

terey's delegates. So too was **Henry W. Halleck,** a bright young lawyer at the time of the convention who was also serving as California's Secretary of State. (Halleck would go on to glory as Chief of Staff for the Union Army in the Civil War.) His major contribution to the state constitution was a measure to protect women's property. Under Halleck's proposal, a woman's property would remain hers after she married, as would any gifts she might receive. This had been a feature of Mexican law, and California was the first U.S. state to include it in its constitution. Halleck, a bachelor, hoped that the measure would attract not just marriageable women to California, but *wealthy* marriageable women. Halleck's name was given to one of the new streets that came into being as Yerba Buena Cove was filled in.

One of San Francisco's delegates who is commemorated in a street name is **Alfred J. Ellis**. He was neither a lawyer nor a general, but was a popular and respected fellow nevertheless: Ellis ran a saloon and boarding house on Montgomery Street. He was also to play an important role as a company commander in the Committees of Vigilance.

The delegates used the constitutions of other states, notably Iowa and New York, as their models. After a month of deliberations, they were able to cobble together a constitution for California and petition the U.S. Congress for admission into the Union as the thirty-first state. Therein lay the difficulty, a headache of Minervan proportions. The Union was evenly divided at that point, with fifteen slave states and fifteen free states. If California were admitted as a free state, the power of the Southern states would be greatly weakened. Southern senators like John C. Calhoun of South Carolina were vehemently opposed. On the other hand, Northern senators, notably **Daniel Webster** of Massachusetts, were just as adamant that California not enter the Union as a slave state, which would tip the balance of power in Congress towards the South.

Into the arena strode **Henry Clay**, America's elder statesman, a veteran of generations of political conflict. Clay proposed a series of measures that he hoped would resolve not only the California question, but also a number of other issues that were dividing the country. In Clay's plan, California would enter as a free state, and the trading of slaves would be prohibited in Washington, D.C. That would please the Northern interests. To keep the Southerners happy, the federal government would assume Texas' public debt; Congress would pass a tough fugitive slave law; and ownership of slaves (though not the buying and selling of them) would be allowed in Washington, D.C. To avoid further political conflict, Utah and New Mexico would be allowed to organize as territories without having to decide for the moment whether slavery would be allowed there.

Henry Clay was known as "The Great Pacificator" for his skill at political negotiation, but he remained stubbornly inflexible on questions of principle. An aide told him that his support of the Compromise of 1850 would probably cost him any chance at the Presidency, but the senator wouldn't budge. In a line never heard from any politician before or since, Clay replied, "I would rather be right than be President." Clay, in fact, had already failed in one bid for that office, in 1844, and had stayed out of public life ever since. Now he was back, newly re-elected to the Senate, and ready to do battle again.

When the Clay Compromise came up for a vote on February 5, 1850, the old man had to be helped up the Senate steps. Once on the Senate floor, he gave an impassioned speech on behalf of California statehood, but even Clay's practiced eloquence was not enough to carry the bill through. The Senate stalled for months, and the debate raged back and forth, often bitterly. Finally, in August, the individual elements of the Clay Compromise were pushed through one at a time, in separate bills, and passed by the Senate. The House approved the measures on September 7, and when **President Millard Fillmore** signed the bills into law two days later, California became the thirty-first state.

All this history was fresh in the minds of the members of a commission, appointed in 1855, to name the new streets in the Western Addition (i.e. west of Larkin Street). The names of many of the politicians who had played a role in California statehood were used, including Senators Henry Clay and Daniel Webster, and President Millard Fillmore. **Franklin Pierce**, who was president at the time the commission met, also had a street named for him.

One of the members of the commission, in contrast to the illustrious national leaders, was a milkman, **Charles Gough**. He made his deliveries on horseback, and was apparently quite a popular figure in the town. When he suggested the idea of naming a street after himself, no one objected, so he went further and named another street for his sister, **Octavia Gough**. Octavia Street and Gough Street run next to each other through the neighborhood where Charles Gough used to deliver fresh milk door-to-door. That area is still known as Cow Hollow, after the dairy cattle that grazed nearby.

California's admission into the Union was the event that everyone had been waiting for since the end of the Mexican-American War. The mail steamer *Oregon* reached San Francisco with the news on October 18, and October 29 was officially set aside as a holiday. The City responded with what the *Annals of San Francisco* called "intense excitement and unprecedented enthusiasm." San Franciscans, who have never needed an excuse to have a party, now had something truly momentous to celebrate, and carnival excitement reigned:

> *Large guns placed upon the Plaza were constantly discharged . . .*
> *Bonfires blazed upon the hills, and rockets were incessantly thrown into the air . . . Some 500 gentlemen and 300 ladies met at the grandest public ball that had yet been witnessed in the city, and danced and made merry till daylight in the pride and joy of their hearts that California was truly now the thirty-first state of the Union.*

In the midst of all the festivities, a chance encounter led to the downfall of one of San Francisco's most respected citizens. A woman who was newly arrived in town approached **Talbot Green** and addressed him as "Mr. Geddis." Bystanders assumed that the stranger was mistaken. Everyone knew Talbot H. Green. He was one of the ruling members of City society, and a close friend to Sam Brannan, William Howard, Jacob Leese, and Thomas O. Larkin. In 1850 San Francisco there were no better connections than those. Green, in fact, had been partners with Larkin in a commercial venture, in Monterey.

The woman was quite insistent. She claimed that the man calling himself Talbot Green was really a Mr. Geddis of Pennsylvania, who had abandoned his wife and five children and disappeared several years before. For his part Green denied everything, and the entire incident probably would have been written-off as a case of mistaken identity, and forgotten were it not for the woman's tenacity. She brought the story to the attention of several newspapers, and try as he would, Green could not make the rumors fade away. Finally he left San Francisco, saying he would return to Pennsylvania, clear his name, and put an end to all these outrageous accusations.

Unfortunately for Talbot Green, the outrageous accusations were true: he really *was* Paul Geddis of Pennsylvania. He had been working in a bank in Philadelphia some years before and had been entrusted to carry $7,000 across town. Along the way, Geddis ran into a poker game, and the bank's fool and the bank's money were soon parted. In desperation, he fled to California, leaving behind his wife and five children. Perhaps he entertained fantasies of making back the money in the gold fields and returning to

Philadelphia in triumph, but that was not to be. When Green (aka Geddis) left San Francisco to "clear his name," his friends expected a speedy return. The passing months, however, were a telling indictment. Word came back that Green was in Pennsylvania, then in Texas, where he was reportedly boasting of his former celebrity status in California. Eventually Green did return to San Francisco, but he was a broken man, friendless and shunned by those whose trusts he had betrayed. Strangely, the name of Green Street was never changed, and the thoroughfare continues to commemorate San Francisco's greatest impostor.

Unlike Green, another Pennsylvania native was enjoying enormous popularity in the City as the 1850's began. President Polk had appointed thirty-year-old **John White Geary**, to serve as San Francisco's first postmaster, in January 1849. When Geary arrived from the East, he brought with him the first regular mail to reach the Bay Area. For the Forty-niners, a letter from home was almost as valuable as gold itself, and the speedy delivery of the mail was a matter of great urgency. It didn't matter that the letters had taken months to get to San Francisco from the East; when the mail did arrive, the citizens didn't want to wait a minute longer than they had to.

Accordingly, Geary and his clerks would stay up all night sorting the mail, with the post office doors locked to keep the impatient crowds outside. Bad weather never dampened their spirits. The *Annals* reported that people thought nothing of "standing all night in the mud, with a heavy rain pouring down upon their heads." Some enterprising souls saw this as a business opportunity just waiting to be exploited, and offered their services as "waiters." They would stand in line all night, fair weather or foul, and their clients would willingly pay as much as twenty dollars for their efforts.

Geary must have done a good job as Postmaster, for in August 1849, he was elected alcalde. His predecessor, Thaddeus Leavenworth, had left him a city in disarray, overwhelmed by Gold Rush immigration and barely functioning as a municipal entity. Geary summed up the state of affairs succinctly when he took office:

> At this time you are without a dollar in the public treasury . . . You have neither an office for your magistrate, nor any other public edifice. You are without a single police officer or watchman, and have not the means of confining a prisoner for an hour . . . Public improvements are unknown in San Francisco.

Geary established a municipal court, organized a paid police force, and bought the *Euphemia* to be used as San Francisco's first city jail. (The *Euphemia* was one of many ships that had been abandoned in Yerba Buena Cove, and as the Cove was filled in, she ended up stranded near the corner of present-day Battery and Jackson Streets.) To pay for these measures, Geary imposed a licensing fee on gambling establishments, a tax that became the largest source of revenue for the City.

John White Geary
San Francisco's 1st Postmaster

Municipal government was further streamlined in May 1850, with the abandonment of the office of alcalde. Under the old Mexican system of administration, the alcalde combined several different functions in one office. The alcalde was similar to the mayor, in that he was the chief executive of the City, but he was also expected to perform other duties as well, akin to a magistrate and justice of the peace. With the phenomenal growth of San Francisco, the more modern office was needed, and Alcalde Geary became Mayor Geary on May 1.

Geary's job title was the least of his troubles. The great scourge of San Francisco in the early 1850s was fire, and not surprisingly. Many of the thousands of immigrants who came in search of Eldorado threw together makeshift shelters from the materials at hand. Too often this meant canvass and spars from the ships that had come around Cape Horn.

Town council ordinances, which were passed in May 1849, prohibited canvass buildings and required property owners to keep six buckets of water handy at all times. These measures were widely ignored and, moreover, proved totally inadequate. A Christmas Eve fire in 1849 did a million dollars worth of damage. Three fires the following year (in May, June, and September) caused damages estimated, altogether, at nearly $7 million.

Worse was yet to come. On May 3, 1851, a fire started to the east of Portsmouth Square and spread north to Broadway and south, as far as Pine Street, before it was controlled the following day. The dozen or so blocks north of Portsmouth Square, which escaped damage in that fire, were consumed in another blaze just a month later.

The problem was not only the use of flammable building materials, but also the lack of any effective means to combat the fires. George Coffin, captain of the *Alhambra*, witnessed the fire of June 14, 1851, from a safe vantage point aboard his ship in the Bay:

> *It was at once seen that nothing could stay the furious element. A fire engine was no more use than an old maid's tea kettle.*

The San Francisco Fire Department Museum at 655 Presidio has a wonderful collection of these old fire engines, one of which dates from 1845. Volunteers pulled the earliest models and pumped them by hand, with as many as fifty people manning the pumps at one time. Horses were added to propel the later units. The firemen in the station house next-door to the museum lovingly maintain the old engines, polishing the gleaming brass pipes, fittings, valves, and gauges. A visit to the museum will give you a sense of the importance that fire played in the early 1850s. It was a time of frequent fires and constant rebuilding. One City lawyer, Joseph Glover Baldwin, boasted that

> *We burn down a city in a night and build it in a day. Contracts for new buildings are signed by the light of the fire that is consuming the old.*

Today San Francisco (whose official seal shows the Phoenix rising from the ashes) still takes fire prevention seriously. Notice as you walk around town that there are different styles and colors of fire hydrants. The small white ones you see on nearly every block are connected to City water, and are adequate in most fires. Larger white hydrants are connected to a separate system of high-pressure water lines that operate independently. Other hydrants have color-coded tops. The ones with blue tops are connected to a large tank on Jones Street on Nob Hill and have sufficient pressure to fight fires up to about one-hundred-and-fifty feet above sea level. Hydrants with red tops draw from an Ashbury Street tank and can be used at higher elevations.

In case an earthquake occurs and ruptures all these water lines, firefighters can still use a system of one-hundred-and-fifty cisterns located underground at key street intersections throughout the City. Each holds at least 75,000 gallons of

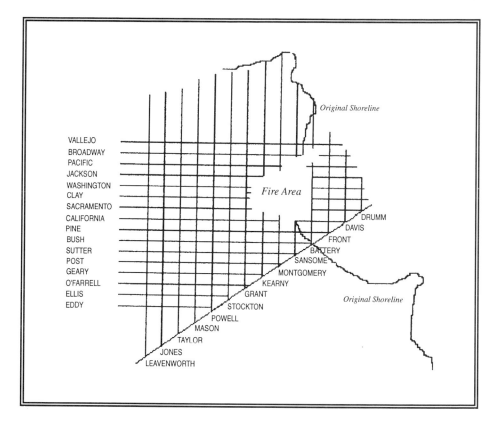

Devastation from the fire of May 4, 1851

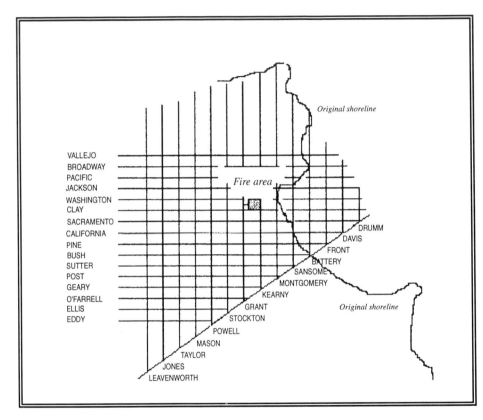

VALLEJO
BROADWAY
PACIFIC
JACKSON
WASHINGTON
CLAY
SACRAMENTO
CALIFORNIA
PINE
BUSH
SUTTER
POST
GEARY
O'FARRELL
ELLIS
EDDY

Original shoreline

Fire area

DRUMM
DAVIS
FRONT
BATTERY
SANSOME
MONTGOMERY
KEARNY
GRANT
STOCKTON
POWELL
MASON
TAYLOR
JONES
LEAVENWORTH

Original shoreline

Devastation from the fire of June 22, 1851

water, some as much as 250,000 gallons. The fire hydrant closest to the cistern is color-coded with a light green top. When you see one of these hydrants, look for a circle or semi-circle of bricks in the adjacent intersection marking the cistern location. Even if the bricks aren't visible (many have been paved-over) there will be a large manhole cover marked "SFFD CISTERN." In a worst-case scenario, firefighters can remove the cover and pump water directly from the cistern.

San Francisco also has one hydrant that is painted gold, at 20th and Church Streets. Following the 1906 earthquake, when virtually all the City's water mains were broken, this hydrant miraculously continued to function. It was used to help stop the flames from advancing any farther into the Mission District. In gratitude, an annual event is held every April 18, when the hydrant is given a fresh coat of gold paint.

You may have noticed that at each City intersection the street names are cast in the sidewalk conrete. This is so that locations can be determined even if some calamity has destroyed the street signs, buildings, and other landmarks. People in charge of clean-

-ing up after fires at various stages of the City's history (especially in 1906) were invariably surprised at how disorienting an urban landscape can be without its familiar buildings. The street names on the sidewalks are intended to help rescue workers navigate the ruins.

John Geary left San Francisco to return to his native Pennsylvania in 1852. (He was to serve as governor of that state from 1867, until his death in 1873.) As a going-away present he gave the City a parcel of land now bounded by Post, Powell, Geary, and Stockton Streets, and the City Council quickly passed a measure that made the land public property in perpetuity. Geary's bequest came to be called Union Square, since it was frequently the site of pro-Union rallies and speeches. The preservation of North and South as one country was the most important political issue debated in the late 1850's in the United States, and newly admitted California, of course, took part.

In San Francisco the national struggle was played out in microcosm in the conflict between two men, **David Broderick** and David Terry. Broderick was a northerner, a Democrat who came West in 1849, from New York, where he had been a ward boss for the Tammany Hall political machine. Broderick speculated in real estate along Yerba Buena Cove, and also established a private mint. He would accept the cumbersome gold dust from miners and melt it down into convenient five- and ten-dollar coins, which were universally accepted by area merchants. The catch was that the five-dollar coins contained only four dollars worth of gold, the ten-dollar coins only eight. Broderick kept the other 20% as his profit.

His real goal was political power, not money. He became a California senator in 1857, and from that office projected his opinions onto the national stage. In particular, Broderick was opposed to the admission of Kansas as a slave state, and spoke out forcefully on the anti-slavery theme.

David Terry was a pro-slavery Southerner whose political career culminated in his appointment to the California Supreme Court. He was hot-tempered and violent, and had been forced to resign his judicial position after stabbing another man in the neck. Collision between Broderick and Terry was inevitable.

While eating breakfast in a San Francisco hotel one morning, Broderick read a newspaper report of one of Terry's speeches. As his temper rose, he blurted out that Terry was a "damned miserable wretch," an opinion overheard by some of Terry's friends at a table nearby. In September 1859, Terry challenged Broderick to a duel.

The two met near the upper end of Lake Merced, at dawn, on the foggy morning of September 13. Both men knew the elaborate formal rituals involved in dueling, and they faithfully observed them. Each brought friends and supporters to act as "seconds," or official go-betweens, and also armorers, witnesses, and a surgeon. In all, nearly eighty people were present. Broderick's surgeon made no attempt to hide the bag of instruments he carried, or the saw that protruded from it in a grisly reminder of what they were about to do. This didn't seem to bother Broderick or Terry. Witnesses reported that both men appeared calm, their Prince Albert coats buttoned up against the morning chill.

Terry provided the weapons, a pair of French dueling pistols with ornate handles, (a fact that was to prove of key importance later). Broderick and Terry walked off the traditional ten paces, turned, and began to raise their pistols. At that moment Broderick's gun went off, and the ball struck the ground just nine feet in front of him. He stood firmly as Terry took aim and fired. The shot caught Broderick in the right side of his chest, and the wound proved fatal three days later.

The Broderick-Terry duel crystallized the entire North-South debate in California into one image. In the public mind, Terry was the villain, Broderick the saint. People said that Terry had practiced extensively with the strange pistols, which Broderick had never seen before. There were rumors that Terry had tampered with Broderick's weapon to cause it to fire prematurely, and many people said that the duel amounted to premeditated murder. Public opinion swung strongly towards the anti-slavery cause. It was even claimed (and widely believed) that Broderick had uttered these improbable final words, "They have killed me because I was opposed to a corrupt administration and the extension of slavery." Broderick's body was placed on a specially constructed platform in Portsmouth Square, where 30,000 mourners came to hear his eulogy.

David C. Broderick in 1856

The man who played Antony to Broderick's Caesar was **Colonel Edward Dickenson Baker,** one of the greatest orators of his day. Baker was a leading organizer of the Republican Party and a close friend of **Abraham Lincoln** from the days when both had practiced law in Illinois. In fact, Lincoln had named one of his sons "Edward Baker Lincoln." It was Baker who introduced Lincoln at the 1861 Republican National Convention, in a hall where an enormous portrait of David Broderick looked down at the assembled delegates. The message was clear. Anti-slavery Democrats who had formerly supported Broderick now rallied behind Lincoln in California, and their backing enabled him to win the election.

Baker spent nine years in San Francisco before moving to Oregon in 1860. He was elected Senator there, but soon resigned in order to lead a company of volunteers in the early days of the Civil War. Baker died in the battle of Ball's Bluff, Virginia, in the fall of 1861. News of his death reached San Francisco via the very first telegraph message sent from the East coast to the West. His body was brought back to San Francisco and buried in Lone Mountain Cemetery near the grave of David Broderick.

For Californians, Baker, like Broderick, became a symbol of noble commitment to principle cut short by tragic death. The two men are memorialized in San Francisco streets that run next to each other, south from the Marina, up over Pacific Heights, and past the site of the old Lone Mountain Cemetery.

Edward Baker
statesman, soldier, and the
greatest orator of his day

Thomas Starr King and his wife

Edward Baker's eulogy was delivered by the greatest preacher of the era, **Thomas Starr King**. King, was a Unitarian minister called from Boston, in 1860, to reinvigor-ate the failing congregation in San Francisco. He wasted no time in setting himself to the task. He preached his first sermon the day after his ship sailed into San Francisco Bay.

By all accounts, Starr King was a human dynamo. Though he stood only five feet tall, and weighed less than 120 pounds, his energy and eloquence impressed all who heard him speak. San Francisco's Unitarian church, where attendance had dwindled for years, was suddenly too small to contain the standing-room-only crowds who came to hear him. Soon a new church was constructed with funds gathered from overflowing collection plates.

Thomas Starr King did not confine his sermons to religious topics. He addressed all the important political and social issues of the day. It seems particularly symbolic that an American flag flew from his church. He called for con-tributions to the Sanitary Commission (a forerunner to the Red Cross) and Californians responded. Nearly one half of all the contributions received by the Sanitary Fund during the war came from California. King spoke out against slavery across the state and north into British Columbia. Large crowds gathered to hear him in Union Square. He visited hospitals, founded a Shakespeare Club, gave public lectures on Socrates and the ancient Greeks, and even spoke to audiences of miners in the Sierra. (He told Jessie Benton Fremont, on one of his many visits to the Fremont's home, "I never knew the exhilaration of public speaking until I faced a front row of revolvers and Bowie knives.")

In a historical coincidence that in hindsight seems pre-destined, Thomas Starr King was also to die tragically, less than three years after he preached at the funeral of Edward Baker. In the Spring of 1864, King complained of a sore throat. It quickly worsened, causing pneumonia and other complications. On March 4, King died. He was just thirty-nine years old. San Francisco again went into mourning. Public buildings were closed, and the state legislature adjourned for three days. As the funeral procession made its way through the City, 20,000 people stood along the route, cannons were fired, and flags flew at half-mast.

In the public mind, King joined Broderick and Baker in a trinity of heroes who represented the very best that the new state had to offer the country. In its first fifteen years California had not only joined the United States, its human talent and energy had played a central role in the preservation of the nation.

The First Unitarian Church is still standing today, a stone and stained glass building at the intersection of Geary and Franklin. Nearby, a short, curving street that connects the Geary Expressway to O'Farrell Street is named Starr King Way in honor of the church's first minister. King Street, three blocks south of Brannan Street, also commemorates the gifted preacher from Boston.

From the time of the state constitutional convention in 1849, until the death of Thomas Starr King in 1864, California went through a dramatic period of growth and

Thomas Starr King

change. San Francisco, underwent a hurried adolescence in those fifteen years, transforming itself from a Gold Rush boomtown into a modern metropolis. In the process, civilized rule of law replaced the rougher system of frontier justice. It was a difficult transition, marked by the breakdown of the old systems of civic order and the emergence of the self-appointed authorities known as the Committees of Vigilance.

CHAPTER 6

The Vigilantes

In the first few years of the Gold Rush, the pattern of San Francisco's early growth was established. Market Street went out towards Mission Dolores through a desert region of sand dunes that were laboriously being shoveled into wagons and dumped in the Cove. South of Market was the chief manufacturing area. The business center was concentrated north of California Street. Rincon Hill (now the much-leveled, western anchorage of the Oakland-Bay Bridge) was considered the best residential district.

San Francisco was the prototypical Boomtown. In 1850 alone, 36,000 people arrived aboard six-hundred-and-fifty-six sailing ships. By the mid-1850s, the City had grown so fast that an "old timer" was anyone who could remember when the Cove came up to Montgomery Street, as it had just a few years before. There were about 40,000 inhabitants, seven-hundred saloons and gambling halls, ten men for every woman, and a crime rate unmatched anywhere else on earth.

A study conducted in 1855 looked back at the previous four years and found that there had been 1,200 murders—an average of five killings every six days. French visitor, Albert Benard de Russailh, was in San Francisco in the spring of 1851, and though he marveled at the many civic improvements, the bright lights on Commercial Street and the brick houses, he also noted that, "hardly an evening passes without drunken brawls during which shots are fired."

Paradoxically, San Francisco was also a civilized place, populated in part by well-educated immigrants with cultured tastes and artistic sensibilities. There were more college graduates in San Francisco than in any other city its size in the United States. They established literary clubs and theater companies, and by 1853 there were twelve newspapers in town.

Unfortunately, the lure of gold had also brought the violent, the desperate, and the depraved from the four corners of the world. For them, as for so many others, the Gold Rush turned out to be more rush than gold. They had little luck in the mountains, much less at the gambling tables, and they quickly turned to crime to sustain themselves.

In the mining camps an *ad hoc* system of rules had evolved to provide some semblance of order. Although these regulations lacked the authority of formal law, they carried the weight of common usage and popular support. It was true that everyone had to fend for himself, but the miners also comprised a social order of their own, one that could be appealed to for justice. By a rough consensus, camp rules were established, disputed claims were settled, and troublemakers were forced to move on.

The miners came down from the hills when the winter rains arrived or when their luck ran out, down from camps with names like: You Bet, Poverty Flat, Henpeck City, Shirt Tail Canyon, Mad Mule, and Last Chance. When they returned to San Francisco, it was to a town in many ways more lawless than the Sierra camps they had just left. San Francisco had no paid police force or municipal courts at all until 1850, and even afterwards corruption and bureaucratic ineptitude frustrated attempts to establish honest government. The City had tried to build a jail to replace the brig, *Euphemia,* for example, but after eleven months and $90,000 only the foundation had been completed. The *Alta California*, the City's largest newspaper, printed blistering editorials against corruption, especially in the judicial system, and lamented that, "our courts, instead of being a terror to evil doers, have proved themselves the protectors of villains, and thus the encouragers of crime."

Gold Rush related problems had surfaced as early as 1849, with a gang of bounty hunters who tracked down runaway sailors. John Henry Brown, proprietor of the Portsmouth House Hotel, reported that captains would pay $25 for each man returned to his ship, and the hunters quickly got out of hand:

> *These men were called the Regulators . . . They were not called Regulators very long, however, as they took a new name and were known as "The Hounds." Some very desperate characters joined the company.*

These "desperate characters" began extorting payoffs from terrified shopkeepers, looting private homes, and robbing people on the streets.

Sacramento Street between Kearny and Montgomery today is a concrete canyon, in the perpetual shadow of towering skyscrapers. Jack's Restaurant, a City landmark since 1864, is the only reminder of Old San Francisco to be found in the area. In the early 1850s, both sides of Sacramento Street were crowded with canvass tents inhabited mostly by foreigners, and this was one of the Hounds' favorite neighborhoods for criminal activity.

Another ill-favored neighborhood was "Little Chile," on the slopes of Telegraph Hill just west of Kearny. The Hounds raided this area on July 15, 1849, raping, beating and stealing with such brazenness that angry citizens demanded action. About twenty of the Hounds were rounded up and tried for conspiracy, riot, robbery, and assault with intent to

Hall McAllister

kill. The prosecutor, **Hall McAllister**, secured convictions against nine of them, and though they were sentenced to long prison terms, the corrupt authorities never carried out the sentences.

The Hounds incident typified the problems that San Francisco would face again later: the arrogant impunity of the criminals; the helpless outrage of the honest citizenry; and the utter incompetence of the duly constituted authorities. These conditions continued unchecked into the 1850's, to the growing exasperation of the City's inhabitants.

On February 19, 1851, merchant Charles J. Jansen was robbed by two men in his store on the corner of Washington and Montgomery Streets, near where the Transamerica Pyramid is now located. Two Australians, Robert Windred and Thomas Berdue, were arrested the next day. Jansen was fairly sure that Berdue was the one who had hit him over the head, and that Windred had been "the short man" with him.

Nearly 1,700 Australians had emigrated to San Francisco in the first half of 1851. A small minority of them were former convicts who had served out their time in British colonial prisons. These "Sydney Ducks," as they were called, provided convenient scapegoats for citizens frustrated by the general lawlessness of the City at that time. Those looking for someone to blame for the crime problem found that Windred and Berdue would fit the bill perfectly. Moreover, the man calling himself Berdue was suspected of being the notorious murderer, James Stuart. Popular sentiment was for immediate hanging.

On February 23, six thousand people crowded into Portsmouth Square, where the Hall of Justice was then located. Mayor John Geary pleaded for order and due process, but the angry crowd very nearly succeeded in wresting the prisoners from the company of militia guarding them. It was only by a concerted effort (and with fixed bayonets) that the guards were able to prevent a mob lynching.

A young merchant, named **William Coleman**, proposed that a popular trial be conducted on the spot, and the elected authorities agreed. This seemed to calm the crowd, who logically assumed that such a trial wouldn't delay the execution for long. At Coleman's urging, twelve jurors were selected, and the impromptu hearing began. Hall McAllister, the prosecutor from the Hounds' trial, acted as defense attorney this time, and again did his job brilliantly. Too brilliantly, some would say. To the disappointment of the crowd, McAllister got the jury to deadlock, nine-to-three because of Jansen's inability to positively identify the two men as his assailants. Ironically, Coleman also contributed to the outcome, by his incompetence in the role of prosecutor. Windred and Berdue were handed back to the police. The official courts then tried, convicted, and jailed them, probably to their great relief.

On May 4, fire destroyed most of San Francisco's business district, nearly twenty-five blocks in all. Fifteen-hundred buildings went up in flames, including every newspaper except the *Alta California*. Arson was suspected, and in fact universally assumed to be the cause. All agreed that the Sydney Ducks were to blame and that the police, of course, would do nothing. Public frustration was reaching the boiling point.

*William Coleman
in 1856*

In early June several merchants met with Sam Brannan, at his offices on the northwest corner of Bush and Sansome streets, just a block south of where the May 3 fire had stopped. (Since 1912, the Union Oil Building, which now houses a branch of California Federal Bank, has stood on the site of Brannan's office.) The outspoken Brannan was the most influential member of San Francisco's "Old Guard." He had been in the City since 1846, when it was still called Yerba Buena; had founded the town's first newspaper, and had nearly single-handedly started the Gold Rush, with his famous march down Montgomery Street. Since that time, Brannan's talent for self-promotion had seldom been idle. He built a diversified empire of real estate and commercial holdings, and could rightly lay claim to being California's first millionaire. The worried merchants who went to see Sam Brannan were confident that he would know what to do.

After several meetings, they decided to form a "Committee of Vigilance." William Coleman was made Chairman, and more than a hundred members signed up in the following few days. The Vigilance Committee issued a statement of purpose, which read in part:

> *We are determined that no thief, burglar, incendiary, or assassin shall escape punishment either by the quibbles of the law, the insecurity of prisons, the carelessness or corruption of the police, or the laxity of those who pretend to administer justice.*

No one, not even the Committee members themselves, seemed to know exactly what this meant in practice, but they didn't have to wait long to find out. On June 10, an English convict named John Jenkins was caught rowing away from Long Wharf, at the foot of Commercial Street, with a stolen safe aboard his dinghy. One of the merchants who gave chase had enrolled as a member of the Vigilance Committee just a few days before. His idea, in which the others concurred, was to hand Jenkins over to the Committee, not to the police.

Jenkins was tried by a hastily convened jury of Vigilantes, found guilty, and sentenced to hang. Justice was swift; in fact, it didn't even wait until daylight. At 1:30 A.M., Jenkins was brought to the Customs House in Portsmouth Square, where a crowd had gathered. A noose was thrown over a roof beam that projected from the old adobe building. Jenkins remained defiant and totally without remorse, asking only for a glass of brandy and a cigar as his last request; these were provided for him. Then there followed an uneasy moment while the crowd considered what to do next. Not surprisingly, it was Sam Brannan who fired them up for the last act of the drama.

"Every lover of liberty and good order lay hold of this rope!" yelled the ex-Mormon Elder. Several men obeyed, Jenkins was hoisted into the air, and in the words of one contemporary account,

> *John Jenkins' body dangled in Portsmouth Square until evening, while the good citizens of San Francisco gesticulated and shouted with joy underneath.*

Of course, Jenkins' execution did nothing to lower the crime rate in San Francisco. (Indeed, one of the men who helped haul Jenkins up the beam had his pocket picked while he was tending the rope.) But at least, the "good citizens of San Francisco" had the satisfaction of doing *something*.

Over the next several weeks the Vigilance Committee met incoming ships, conducted brief interviews with the passengers, and decided whether the newcomers could stay. They also made sweeps through "Sidneytown," a predominantly Australian enclave east of Kearny between Broadway and Union Street. All this was done quite openly, and while some people objected to the Committee's methods, few were seriously opposed to its existence.

On one of its sweeps through Sidneytown early in July, the Committee arrested an Australian calling himself William Stephens, who bore an amazing resemblance to Thomas Berdue, the man everyone thought was James Stuart.

Adding to the confusion, Berdue/Stuart was at that moment being tried in Marysville for crimes he was accused of committing there. Under questioning, "Stephens" admitted being the real James Stuart, and confessed to the robbery of Jansen's store back in February. Berdue was exonerated and released. Windred, "the short man," had already escaped from jail and disappeared from the pages of history. On July 11, James Stuart was marched to the end of the Market Street Wharf and hanged in front of a huge crowd.

The following month the Committee sentenced two more men to death. In this case the uneasy coexistence between the Vigilantes and the official authorities turned into open conflict. Robert McKenzie and Samuel Wittaker had been arrested by the Vigilantes, tried, and locked away in the Committee holding cell awaiting execution. San Francisco's mayor, **Charles Brenham**, ordered Sheriff John Hays to rescue them. In a daring raid, the former Texas Ranger broke into the Committee rooms in the middle of the night and transferred Wittaker and McKenzie to the county jail, on the north side of Broadway between Kearny and DuPont. (The old jail was on the same block as today's Condor Club, made famous by a silicone-inflated Carol Doda in the 1960s.)

Wittaker and McKenzie were not safe for long. Just four days later, a large force of Vigilantes swooped down on the jail and rushed the two men back across town, to their headquarters on Sansome Street near Bush. They were immediately hung from the second floor windows there, with a large crowd again in attendance. One eyewitness wrote:

More than 15,000 gathered to witness the double hanging. When all was over, the crowds drifted away, praising the conduct of the Vigilance Committee . . . it is an excellent institution.

New members continued to join, impressed with the bold decisiveness of the group. The Committee eventually had seven-hundred-and-ten members, drawn mainly from the merchant class of successful, well-educated property owners. Long-time residents, Jacob Leese and William Howard, joined. Howard's former partner, Henry Mellus, and Constitutional Convention delegate, Alfred J. Ellis, were also members. Even **Henry Haight**, who later as Governor established the University of California, was one of the Vigilantes.

Many other people from the Vigilante era are also recalled in the names of City streets. McAllister Street runs from the University of San Francisco, eastward to Market Street past City Hall, where there is a statue of Georgia native, Hall McAllister. Hardly a blood-thirsty anarchist (as some would characterize the Vigilantes), McAllister was a vestry man for the San Francisco Adventist Church, where his brother, F. Marion McAllister, was the pastor. The pedestal of the City Hall statue pays tribute to the brilliant lawyer with the following inscription:

Hall McAllister
Leader of the California Bar
Learned Able Eloquent
A Fearless Advocate
A Courteous Foe

The Committee's secretary, **Isaac Bluxome**, has a street named for him one block south of Brannan Street. Bluxome, too, was a solid pillar of society. Like McAllister, he had been active in the fight against the Hounds. Later he gave

away more than five-hundred books, a generous donation that became the nucleus of an early collection known as the Mechanic's Library. William T. Coleman, the Committee's chairman, was also a community member of some stature. He had married the daughter of Daniel Page, former mayor of St. Louis and founder of a leading San Francisco banking house. Coleman is commemorated at Coleman Street, in Hunter's Point.

Charles Brenham, who served as mayor after John White Geary's term expired, was honored in Brenham Place, a short lane that ran along the west side of Portsmouth Square. Recently the name of this street was changed to "Walter U. Lum Place," to honor a civic leader, but Brenham wasn't forgotten entirely: a one-block section of Seventh Street north of Market now bears his name. And merchant **Charles Jansen**, victim of the robbery that started the Vigilante episode, can claim immortality in a tiny lane that connects Lombard to Greenwich, between Taylor and Mason Streets.

On September 16, 1851, the Committee of Vigilance suspended their operations. During their one-hundred days in power they had forced ninety-one people to come before them for hearings. Forty-one people were dismissed. Fourteen people were strongly urged to leave town, and fourteen others were banished by placing them on ships bound for distant places. Jenkins, Stuart, Wittaker and McKenzie were hanged, and one man was publicly flogged. The rest were turned over to the legal authorities.

A dangerous precedent had been set. Honest citizens, having sampled the ruthless efficiency of mob rule once, were strongly tempted to return to it. Within a few years, the Vigilance Committee would reconvene. Two incidents brought this about.

The first happened in late 1855. General William Richardson was one of 2,000 people present at the American Theater, on November 15, to see the world premiere of *Nicodemus; or The Unfortunate Fisherman*. Sitting directly behind him was professional gambler, Charles Cora, accompanied by his mistress, a notorious madam named Belle. Richardson was a federal Marshall, an officer in the state militia, and a Southern gentleman of conservative moral tastes, and he loudly objected to the presence of the couple behind him. Violence was avoided for the moment, but two days later Richardson confronted Cora at the Blue Wing Saloon on Montgomery Street. Cora went outside, shots were fired, and Richardson fell dead near the corner of Clay and Leidesdorff streets.

In the trial that followed, Cora was able to hire (with Belle's nearly unlimited financial backing) the best lawyers money could buy. They convinced the jury that Richardson had been the aggressor, and Cora went free. The public was outraged, but was helpless to do anything about it.

The other incident that led to the Second Committee of Vigilance was the killing of a man who called himself James King of William. (Back in his native Maryland, King had arrived at this strange name by adding his father's name,

James King of William

William, to his surname to distinguish himself from the many other James Kings.) As "James King of William" he had come West and had tried his hand at a number of occupations in banking, without notable success. Looking around for a way to make his living, he decided to start a newspaper, and the first issue of the *Evening Bulletin* appeared on October 8, 1855. King of William immediately launched attacks on lawlessness, corruption, gambling, and vice in general. He was a man of many opinions, all of them strongly held, and the *Bulletin* frequently adopted the tone of a holy crusade. King of William's brand of outspoken self-righteousness proved very popular, and readership grew rapidly.

Less than a year after the first issue was published, King of William was on the trail of James P. Casey, whose recent election to the Board of Supervisors had involved some clumsy but effective ballot box stuffing. Articles in the *Bulletin* played up the fact that Casey had served time in Sing Sing Prison, in New York, an accomplishment that Casey was hoping to keep quiet about. In a rage, he shot King of William, on May 14, 1856, as he left the *Bulletin* offices on Montgomery Street near Commercial, less than a block from where Cora shot Richardson.

While King of William lingered near death, William Coleman called for a public meeting to discuss the twin outrages of King of William's shooting and Cora's acquittal. Most of the people who had been members of the first Committee of Vigilance responded, in addition to many new recruits. As in the first Committee, each man was sworn to secrecy and given a number to protect his identity. (Coleman was Number 1.) Just two days later, member number 2,500 was sworn in; membership ultimately reached more than 6,000.

They adopted as their symbol an open, ever-watchful eye and established their headquarters at 41 Sacramento Street, between Front and Davis. The building was fortified with sandbags piled in long, high rows and became known as "Fort Gunnybags." Today the site of Fort Gunnybags is across the street from Embarcadero Two, a retail and office complex. There is no building there now, only an empty lot, but a bronze plaque, complete with the all-seeing eye, marks the location.

Committee of Vigilance Symbol

F.C.BOYD.

Published by the *NOISY CARRIER'S BOOK AND STATIONERY CO.*, 87 *Battery Street, San Francisc*

FORT VIGILANTE.
Showing the defences around the "Vigilant Committee Rooms."

Fort Gunnybags was also referred to as Fort Vigilante.
Its Committee rooms were well-defended.

The Second Committee of Vigilance differed from the first in several ways, most notably in their enormous numbers and heavy armament. The Vigilantes' forces included 4,000 infantrymen, armed with muskets; and four, 100-man companies of artillery, with thirty cannons, many of them donated by ships in the Cove. Two cavalry companies and several companies of "irregulars" rounded out the group. The entire operation was run with military discipline. Each company had its commander (Alfred J. Ellis led one company), and between the daily practice drills and the nights spent on patrol, being a Vigilante was a full-time job.

The Second Committee, unlike the first, faced some serious opposition from establishment politicians. These worthies, marching under the banner of the "Law and Order Party," blustered with indignation that the Vigilantes would try to usurp power from them. The Law and Order Party, however, was made up mainly of people with a vested interest in the status quo, and their motives are open to question.

In the summer of 1856, writer, **Prentice Mulford**, was living in a room across Sacramento Street from Fort Gunnybags. Mulford was a sharp observer of the scene around him. His book, *Prentice Mulford's Story*, colorfully captures the flavor of the times. He described the City as "fog in the morning, dust and wind in the afternoon, and the Vigilance Committee the rest of the time." He was not particularly enamored of the Vigilantes, but he spoke even less highly of

> the "Law and Order" men, who were not "orderly" at all, but who had captured the city's entire governmental and legal machinery and ran it to suit their own purposes.

The stage was set for the inevitable clash between the two groups competing for control of the City. One of the Vigilante leaders who was to play a leading role in the confrontation was **Miers F. Truett**. His name is not well known today, though he is remembered in Truett Street, an alley just uphill from the Chinatown Recreation Center on Mason Street, near the Cable Car Barn. He and William Coleman led 2,500 armed Vigilantes to the county jail on Broadway, where Cora and Casey were being held. City officials there were hoping to bolster their claim to legitimacy by keeping custody of the two men, but Truett and Coleman had a very convincing argument of their own: they formed their troops into ranks along Broadway and leveled a cannon at the front door of the jail. The authorities inside wisely turned Cora and Casey over to them without resistance.

On May 19, the trial began at Fort Gunnybags. Truett served as defense attorney, but the verdict was never really in doubt, especially when word reached them that King of William had died. As his last request, Cora was allowed to marry Belle in the Committee rooms after the expected sentence was announced. Three days later, while King of William's funeral was being held, Casey and Cora were hung from the second-story windows of Fort Gunnybags.

San Francisco's mayor, **James Van Ness**, arrived from his native Vermont a few years earlier and immediately jumped into City politics as a Supervisor. He had been in San Francisco during the First Committee's reign, and sensed the direction events were taking now. Van Ness appealed to Governor J. Neely Johnson, who arranged to meet quietly with William Coleman and discuss the situation.

Their meeting gives an interesting insight into the Vigilantes' goals and methods. Years later (November 1891) Coleman wrote his reminiscences in *Century* magazine, and he explained that the Vigilantes' purpose was

> to see that the laws were executed upon a few prominent criminals whom the officers of the law had allowed to go unpunished; to drive away from the State some notoriously bad characters; to purify the atmosphere morally and politically, and then to disband.

Cora and Casey are hung from the second floor windows of Fort Gunnybags.

Coleman spelled out what he thought the respective roles of the Vigilantes and the government should be. He had told the Governor to

> *Do your duty in issuing your proclamations and manifestos, and maintaining formally the dignity of the law, but leave to us the work, and we shall get through with it in a short time and quit, and quite gladly.*

After the Cora/Casey hangings, the Second Committee of Vigilance got down to "the work," going after the same elements that King of William had railed against in the *Bulletin*. They targeted gamblers, arsonists, street ruffians, ballot box stuffers, crooked politicians, and all classes of real or suspected villains. Over the next few months, twenty-five "undesirables" were placed aboard outbound sailing ships and warned not to return. Five others were spared the long ocean voyage and were simply told to leave town. Perhaps as many as eight hundred other people left San Francisco voluntarily without waiting to be told.

That seemed to take care of "the work," and many of the Vigilantes thought it was time to disband. Unfortunately, this proved to be a lot more difficult than they had imagined. Governor Johnson had declared San Francisco to be in a state of insurrection on June 3. He had asked President Pierce to send federal troops to San Francisco, and though Pierce refused, he did authorize the federal garrison at Benicia to release one hundred muskets to the state militia.

On June 19, the Vigilantes intercepted the shipment aboard the schooner, *Julia,* and made off with the weapons. Shortly thereafter, a Vigilante named Sterling Hopkins was stabbed in the neck by Law and Order man David S. Terry, who was a judge on the State Supreme Court. When the Committee seized Terry and held him for trial, events were spinning out of control. It was one thing to deport petty criminals, or even to hang them, but to abduct a State Supreme Court Judge was another matter entirely. The City held its collective breath as the Vigilante trial of Judge Terry began. Would the Vigilantes have the nerve to hang him? Would the Governor send in the militia? For that matter, would President Pierce send in the Army? San Francisco teetered on the edge of total chaos.

For weeks, the trial dragged on, with no sign of resolution. The hero of the hour turned out to be, as no one would have guessed, the Vigilantes' surgeon. This was prominent City doctor, **R. Beverly Cole**, for whom Cole Street in the Haight Ashbury district is named. Cole had earlier attended James King of William, who unfortunately had been beyond help. Under Cole's care, Hopkins miraculously recovered. This provided the face-saving way out that everyone had been hoping for. Terry agreed to leave San Francisco, and the Vigilantes in turn agreed to let the matter drop.

On that note, the Committee of Vigilance felt that its mission to clean up the City was done, at least for the time being, and the better part of valor now was to disband. In a final parade, on August 18, 6,000 armed members marched through San Francisco in military fashion before hanging up their muskets and returning to their mundane civilian lives.

The Vigilante episode marked an important turning point in the history of San Francisco, the difficult transition from Gold Rush boomtown to modern metropolis. No one was more representative of this era than Sam Brannan, principle organizer of the Vigilante groups. Brannan was a living bridge between sleepy Yerba Buena, with its eight hundred residents, and the cosmopolitan giant that materialized on the shores of the Bay almost overnight.

The wealth of the Gold Rush, which had once seemed inexhaustible, ended in just a few years; in 1855 there was a banking panic and an economic recession that left a third of the City's 1,000 shops empty. Silver strikes in the Comstock Lode, in 1859, carried San Francisco to new and even greater prosperity, but in the 1870s, a flood of cheap manufactured goods, caused by the newly-completed, transcontinental railroad, drove down prices and caused wide scale unemployment.

Brannan's fortunes followed the same pattern. He was nearing the height of his powers as the Second Committee disbanded and the rule of law returned, and San Francisco was soon too tame for him. Brannan was a pioneer, not a settler; a blazer of trails, not a paver of roads. In 1859, the forty-year-old Brannan bought a large parcel of land in Napa county, about eighty miles northeast of San Francisco. At the geysers and hot springs there he tried to develop a resort that would rival the fashionable spas on the east coast. It would be the Saratoga of California, or "Calistoga," as Brannan accidentally christened it one day after too many drinks.

Calistoga never attracted enough visitors to turn a profit, and the vast business empire Brannan had built up over the years started falling apart. His wife, Eliza, sued for divorce, and her lawyers demanded that her half of the estate be turned over in cash. The river ferries, the real estate holdings, the bank certificates, the railroad investments, the silver lands in Nevada, all were liquidated at ruinous prices.

Brannan had one great dream left in him, a colonizing scheme in northern Mexico. President Díaz had given him nearly two million acres of land in Sonora as payment for loans he had made to the Juárez government in its fight against Maximillian. Brannan, the visionary who brought a group of Mormon colonists to Yerba Buena in 1846, hoped to repeat the miracle in Mexico nearly forty years later. For the last ten years of his life, he struggled both with the Mexican bureaucracy and with reluctant American investors, but the dream was not to be. He died in May 1889, with none of the estimated $5 million dollar fortune that had once been his. His grave marker reads:

Sam Brannan 1819-1889
California Pioneer of '46
Dreamer, Leader and Empire Builder

Brannan's death marked the symbolic end of the old San Francisco, the Gold Rush city of frontier justice and Vigilantes. It seems ironic that James Marshall, who found the first gold nugget, John Sutter, on whose land the gold was found, and Sam Brannan, who gave the news to the world, all died penniless.

CHAPTER 7

The Earthquake

The *Annals of San Francisco*, written in 1855, report that earthquakes rocked San Francisco in 1812, 1829, and 1839. The 1812 earthquake was particularly severe, and was felt over most of California. The *Annals* go on to say:

> Since these dates, no serious occurrences of this nature have happened at San Francisco, though almost every year slight shocks, and occasionally smarter ones have been felt. God help the city if any great catastrophe of this nature should ever take place!

Other earthquakes did take place, of course, notably on October 8, 1865, and October 21, 1868. Several chimneys and cornices fell, plaster cracked, and a few people even died. There was no great mystery to it: earthquakes would always be as much a part of San Francisco life as the fog that rolled in on summer afternoons.

Probably no one appreciated the full implications of San Francisco's unique geology until the early morning of April 18, 1906, when *the* earthquake struck. Officially, the force of that quake is estimated at 8.25 on the Richter scale, and its duration is usually listed at forty-eight seconds. There is some disagreement on these numbers, but everyone who lived through the quake agreed on the unofficial measurements: it was big, and it lasted an eternity.

Landfilling operations in San Francisco began with the "water lots," of Jasper O'Farrell's 1847 Survey, and had proceeded more or less continuously since that time. By the time of the 1906 earthquake, nearly 20% of the City's 410,000 inhabitants lived on landfill, or as it was then called, "made ground." Not surprisingly, the greatest destruction was to be found in those areas. At Howard Street near Eighteenth, where the old Mission Creek had been filled-in, geologic forces caused the ground to liquefy. Houses sank as much as two stories, leaning against each other at alarming angles. The former swamp area at Sixth

Houses on Howard Street between 17th and 18th streets

Dozens died when the four-story Valencia Street Hotel sank into "made ground." Victims drowned in water from a broken main before rescuers could reach them.

and Folsom was also particularly hard-hit. Within a hundred-foot radius of that intersection, at least fifty people died in the first few minutes of the disaster.

Fires erupted almost instantly from broken gas lines and toppled chimneys. At least forty buildings were aflame within fifteen minutes of the first shock, but as bad as it was, it would have been far worse had the earthquake struck an hour later. Not many people were awake at 5:12 A.M., and so, fortunately, not many wood stoves were in use at the time of impact. Even so, fires broke out along Market Street and in the Mission.

In 1905, San Francisco's fire department had been evaluated by the Fire Underwriters, who found a number of weak spots in its defenses. Many of the thirty-eight engines weren't capable of pumping at their rated capacities, for example. Also, the City's fifty-seven underground cisterns dated to the 1850s; many were dry or choked with debris, and their locations were not clearly marked. The department relied on the memories of a few old-time firefighters to find them.

Still, there was reason for pride in the department as well. A new central alarm system had recently been installed, the equipment was up-to-date, and the personnel were well trained. Even the horses that pulled the fire engines were kept in peak physical condition, with half-hour exercise periods, twice a day. Response times were remarkably quick. By an ingenious system of pulleys and counterweights, the collars and harnesses could be lowered onto the animals and attached in a matter of a few seconds. (San Francisco converted to gasoline-powered engines, over a ten-year period, starting in 1912.)

Even the latest equipment was of no use, given the magnitude of the disaster; the firemen never really had a chance. Some of the station houses collapsed, trapping fire engines inside. Horses ran off in terror, telephones went dead, and the new alarm system was knocked out. The fire chief, Dennis Sullivan, was fatally injured by falling masonry in the first moments of the earthquake. Lacking their communication system, much of their equipment, and their chief, some firemen were nevertheless able to respond to the initial fires. To their horror, they found that there was no water at the hydrants; ground motion had severed most of the mains. Now what?

The Army's Pacific Division Commander at the time was General Frederick Funston. He had begun his military career, improbably, as a botanist, gathering plant specimens from Death Valley, and Alaska, for the Department of Agriculture. When the Spanish-American War broke out in 1896, five-foot-two, "Fearless Freddie" Funston had led the Twentieth Kansas Regiment to glory, in the Battle of Calumpit, in the Philippines. He captured an insurgent leader, Emilio Aguinaldo, and was awarded the Congressional Medal of Honor for his exploits. Now just forty years old, Funston could already look back on a fine career. Little did he realize, on that April morning in 1906, that his greatest challenge was still ahead of him.

Funston was living in a house at Jones and Washington Streets. When the first tremor knocked him out of bed, he did what any military man would do, he headed for the nearest high ground. In this case that meant Nob Hill, just three blocks to the south. From there Funston could see damaged buildings and the first fires breaking out along the south side of Market Street. It was obvious to him that extraordinary measures would be needed to save the City. He had his carriage driver race to the Presidio with orders to send troops. In a few hours, Funston had 1,500 men at his command.

The civilian authorities, meanwhile, were gathering at Portsmouth Plaza in the Hall of Justice building. Mayor Eugene Schmitz met with a group of prominent citizens who later became known as the Committee of Fifty, and they plotted a course of action. Schmitz had seen some looting on his way to the meeting, and though it was not within his legal authority to do so, he ordered that looters be shot on sight. He also ordered that all liquor stores and saloons be closed and that any readily-available stocks of liquor destroyed. It was hoped that these measures would help maintain control of the situation, but they were only marginally effective. Drunkenness in the next few days, both civilian and military, was not uncommon, and records show that six people were shot for looting.

The Great Fire began as dozens of smaller fires that later merged. One was working its way along Market Street, heading southwest. It reached the Grand Opera House on

General Frederick Funston

85

Mission Street, where Enrico Caruso had sung with the New York Opera Company the night before. The lavish hall, which boasted the world's largest crystal chandelier, was utterly consumed, along with all the elaborate sets and costumes. Cleanup workers would later find a large lump of blackened glass, all that remained of the elegant chandelier.

On Market Street, near Second, the Grand Hotel burned, raining sparks onto the roof of the Palace Hotel, just across New Montgomery Street. Banking tycoon, **William Ralston,** had built the eight-hundred-room Palace in the late 1860's, and it was the most opulent hotel in America at the time. Everything was done on a fabulous scale: a grand entrance allowed carriages to drive into a central courtyard that rose seven stories, to a vaulted glass roof; seven thousand windows wrapped around the building; thirty bartenders kept the liquor flowing in the enormous bar.

Ralston had also spent millions to make the Palace earthquake- and fire-proof. Tons of iron banding were supposed to allow the brick walls to withstand earthquakes. A 350,000 gallon cistern, beneath the courtyard, would provide water in the event of fire, as would roof tanks that were connected to private hydrants down on the sidewalks in front of the hotel. But none of these measures would save the Palace in 1906. The earthquake struck the building with a kind of twisting motion, causing major structural damage, and firemen used all the water in the Palace cisterns to fight the fire further up Market Street. By the time the flames reached Ralston's hotel, there was nothing to do but watch.

Another blaze, in Hayes Valley, came to be called the "Ham and Eggs" Fire. Supposedly it was started by a woman cooking breakfast for her husband late Wednesday morning. Their earthquake-damaged chimney set the roof on fire, and the flames quickly spread east towards City Hall. Next door at the Mechanics' Pavilion, in the block bounded by Hayes, Grove, Polk, and Larkin, an emergency hospital was set-up to treat the thousands of injured. It was thought to be a safe refuge from the inferno downtown. Patients from the badly-damaged, Central Emergency Hospital had been moved here in the first hours after the quake, but as the Ham and Eggs Fire rapidly approached, everyone had to be moved again. Rescue workers barely succeeded in saving the 354 patients in their care. The fire traveled so quickly that some twenty dead had to be left behind to the flames.

Also relocated to the Mechanics' Pavilion was the magnificent collection of rare books that the late Mayor, **Adolph Sutro,** had bequeathed to the City. It included nearly 250,000 items: priceless Renaissance manuscripts from Europe and Elizabethan England, as well as rare California maps and pamphlets from the Spanish and Mexican periods. The collection had been housed in three separate locations around the City. The Montgomery Block (now the site of the Transamerica Pyramid) held most of it. As the flames closed in on that neighborhood, everything there was hauled by wagon to the Mechanics' Pavilion for safekeeping. Ironically, the Montgomery Block was the only large downtown building to survive the fire, but by early Wednesday afternoon the Mechanics' Pavilion and much of the Sutro Collection were ashes.

The Montgomery Block was the only large, downtown building to survive the fire.

A group poses in front of the ruins of City Hall

City Hall

A third major fire began in Delmonico's Restaurant, at 110 O'Farrell Street, near Powell, possibly set accidentally by soldiers cooking, or according to another story, deliberately set by an enemy of the building's owner. In either case, it marked the beginning of the end. Until early Wednesday afternoon, there had been some hope that the fire might be contained. The north side of Market Street, from Taylor up to Kearny, was still safe, including Union Square and the surrounding retail shopping district. With the outbreak of the Delmonico Fire, however, all was lost. By Thursday, the fire had swept through the Union Square area and headed up Nob Hill. The Ham and Eggs Fire, meanwhile, crossed Market Street between Eighth and Ninth Streets, fanned by a west wind. When it joined the Delmonico Fire to the east, there were no longer several distinct fires, there was only "The Fire," a conflagration that threatened to envelop the entire City.

Soldiers and firemen fought it on several fronts. At the end of Market Street, fireboats and the Navy destroyer, *Preble,* used their pumps to save the earthquake-shattered Ferry Building, where thousands of terrified City residents were boarding boats for the East Bay and Marin County. Using salt water from the Bay, firefighters contained the flames along Main Street on the East and Townsend Street on the South.

General Funston, meanwhile, surveyed the firestorm from its western edge as it approached him in a front nearly a mile wide. In a meeting with Mayor Schmitz and the Committee of Fifty, on Thursday morning, Funston had argued forcefully for dynamiting a firebreak fifty yards wide along

Delmonico's Restaurant at 110 O'Farrell Street in 1906
Building at far right was where one fire started on Wednesday afternoon.

Dewey Monument in Union Square - April 1906

Dewey Monument in Union Square today

Smoke from the Great Fire was visible for many miles.

A horse-drawn fire engine waits and crowds watch as smoke advances towards them.

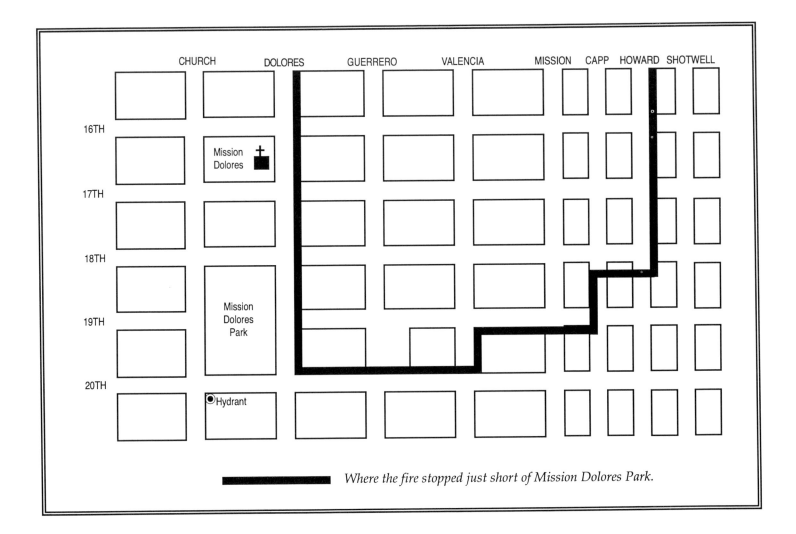

CHURCH DOLORES GUERRERO VALENCIA MISSION CAPP HOWARD SHOTWELL

16TH

Mission
Dolores

17TH

18TH

Mission
Dolores
Park

19TH

20TH

Hydrant

Where the fire stopped just short of Mission Dolores Park.

the eastern side of Van Ness Avenue, from Golden Gate Avenue north to Sacramento Street. The use of dynamite entailed its own hazards: frequently the explosions started new fires or blew flaming debris into unburned areas. But crude as it was, dynamite was the only weapon Funston had, and Van Ness Avenue seemed like the best place to use it. Van Ness is the widest street in San Francisco. Funston knew that if the fire couldn't be stopped there, it would burn out-of-control into the Western Addition and might well destroy the Presidio and Fort Mason. Reluctantly, Mayor Schmitz agreed to the desperate plan.

At about three o'clock Thursday, soldiers herded people north on Van Ness and began dynamiting, and setting backfires, to create a firebreak. As if possessed of a malevolent intelligence, the firestorm moved north in a flanking maneuver, the wind pushing it relentlessly. Between Clay and Sutter, the fire actually crossed Van Ness and spread one block west to Franklin, but dynamiting along Franklin, and later Gough, held it in check. A hose was run from the Army tug, *General Slocum*, at Fort Mason, up Van Ness all the way to Sacramento Street, nearly a mile away. Between the dynamiting, the water from the *General Slocum*'s pumps, and a favorable change in the wind, Funston's forces began to get the upper hand. It was a narrow escape, but by dawn on Friday morning the Western Addition was out of danger.

The battle was far from over, however. The same shift in the wind that had earlier seemed such a blessing now sent the fire roaring towards North Beach. Nearly 30,000 people were trapped along the waterfront between Fort

Mason and Pier 27, at the end of Lombard. Every vessel that could float was pressed into service, ferries, tugs, Italian fishing boats, even Chinese junks, in a monumental rescue effort. Against the backdrop of a towering wall of black smoke that rose thousands of feet into the air, the Dunkirk-style operation successfully plucked everyone from the beaches and piers on the City's northern waterfront. By noon on Saturday, the northern edge of fire was out.

While Funston was fighting to save the Western Addition, another group was valiantly battling the inferno in the Mission District. Thousands of refugees fleeing the fire had gathered in Mission Dolores Park, two blocks south of the old Mission. It was here that the fire would have to be stopped, along the wide thoroughfare of Dolores Street. If not, the flames would almost certainly devour the entire Mission area (composed mainly of wood-frame buildings) gather speed as they moved uphill to Twin Peaks, and continue unchecked all the way to the ocean.

Army dynamite teams worked frantically to destroy buildings in the fire's path. They were joined by thousands of civilian volunteers, who razed smaller structures without the need for explosives. In teams of a hundred or more people, they managed to physically pull down the houses with heavy ropes fastened to the corners of the buildings. It was a noble effort, but it probably wouldn't have been enough except for a piece of remarkable luck: when someone tried the hydrant at 20th and Church Street, it was found to be working. Firemen quickly struggled to move two engines up Dolores Street, to 20th, but the steep hill and the heavy

Where the Fire stopped. A view towards downtown from Dolores Park.

loads were too much for their exhausted horses. Again hundreds of volunteers joined in and succeeded in pushing the pumpers up to the hydrant. Hoses were then run downhill to the battle line on Mission Street.

The fire, nearly four blocks wide, approached Dolores Park from the northeast. Temperatures within the inferno reached 2,700 degrees Fahrenheit, sufficient to melt steel and glass. Large flaming cinders exploded outward and upward from the front, landing on rooftops and on the refugees huddled in the park. A wall of invisible poison gas advanced ahead of the flames. Then the front of the Great Fire itself arrived, making a rumbling, ground-shaking noise that witnesses described as sounding like a locomotive. No one had any illusions about the seriousness of the task ahead, or about the consequences of failure.

If the San Francisco earthquake and fire had a finest hour, this may have been it. With dampened burlap bags, bed sheets, and mops, nearly 3,000 volunteers, Army troops, and what was left of the Fire Department, fought for seven hours to save the City. Men held doors in front of them as shields and ran forward to beat back the flames and cinders. As they were overcome by the heat, smoke, and gas, other volunteers would take their place. By late Friday night there was cause for hope; refugees in higher vantage points could see the fire begin to grow dimmer. By early Saturday morning, the greatest urban fire in history had burned itself out.

In its wake were more than four square miles of devastation, about 28,000 ruined buildings. The U.S. Post Office at Seventh and Mission survived, as did the old Mint at Fifth and Mission, though its windows had melted. A few other areas, notably Jackson Square, the Montgomery Block, and the summits of Russian Hill and Telegraph Hill, were also saved, but everywhere else within the fire zone the destruction was total.

The scale of the catastrophe is difficult to grasp. More than ten million yards of rubble had to be cleared before rebuilding could even begin. Much of it was hauled out to sea in barges, dumped into Mission Bay (just north of China Basin at the end of King Street), or used as fill along the shoreline in other parts of the City. The Palace Hotel alone required 15,000 wagon loads to haul away its thirty-million bricks. (What was once the grandest hotel in America is now landfill at Aquatic Park.)

The earthquake brought out the best and the worst in people. There were tales of great heroism and of shameless cowardice, of personal sacrifice and of petty selfishness. Frederick Funston was widely regarded as the savior of the City, not without reason. San Francisco's, un-numbered Thirteenth Avenue, which runs from the Presidio to Golden Gate Park, is today called Funston Avenue. In Fort Mason there is a Funston Road, and in the Presidio another Funston Avenue. The public park between Bay and Chestnut

St. Francis Hotel and Union Square, 1906

Looking towards Market on O'Farrell Street.

The Call=Chronicle=Examiner

SAN FRANCISCO, THURSDAY, APRIL 19, 1906.

EARTHQUAKE AND FIRE:
SAN FRANCISCO IN RUINS

DEATH AND DESTRUCTION HAVE BEEN THE FATE OF SAN FRANCISCO. SHAKEN BY A TEMBLOR AT 5:13 O'CLOCK YESTERDAY MORNING, THE SHOCK LASTING 48 SECONDS, AND SCOURGED BY FLAMES THAT RAGED DIAMETRICALLY IN ALL DIRECTIONS, THE CITY IS A MASS OF SMOULDERING RUINS. AT SIX O'CLOCK LAST EVENING THE FLAMES SEEMINGLY PLAYING WITH INCREASED VIGOR, THREATENED TO DESTROY SUCH SECTIONS AS THEIR FURY HAD SPARED DURING THE EARLIER PORTION OF THE DAY. BUILDING THEIR PATH IN A TRIANGUAR CIRCUIT FROM THE START IN THE EARLY MORNING, THEY JOCKEYED AS THE DAY WANED, LEFT THE BUSINESS SECTION, WHICH THEY HAD ENTIRELY DEVASTATED, AND SKIPPED IN A DOZEN DIRECTIONS TO THE RESIDENCE PORTIONS. AS NIGHT FELL THEY HAD MADE THEIR WAY OVER INTO THE NORTH BEACH SECTION AND SPRINGING ANEW TO THE SOUTH THEY REACHED OUT ALONG THE SHIPPING SECTION DOWN THE BAY SHORE, OVER THE HILLS AND ACROSS TOWARD THIRD AND TOWNSEND STREETS. WAREHOUSES, WHOLESALE HOUSES AND MANUFACTURING CONCERNS FELL IN THEIR PATH. THIS COMPLETED THE DESTRUCTION OF THE ENTIRE DISTRICT KNOWN AS THE "SOUTH OF MARKET STREET." HOW FAR THEY ARE REACHING TO THE SOUTH ACROSS THE CHANNEL CANNOT BE TOLD AS THIS PART OF THE CITY IS SHUT OFF FROM SAN FRANCISCO PAPERS.

AFTER DARKNESS, THOUSANDS OF THE HOMELESS WERE MAKING THEIR WAY WITH THEIR BLANKETS AND SCANT PROVISIONS TO GOLDEN GATE PARK AND THE BEACH TO FIND SHELTER. THOSE IN THE HOMES ON THE HILLS JUST NORTH OF THE HAYES VALLEY WRECKED SECTION PILED THEIR BELONGINGS IN THE STREETS AND EXPRESS WAGONS AND AUTOMOBILES WERE HAULING THE THINGS AWAY TO THE SPARSELY SETTLED REGIONS. EVERYBODY IN SAN FRANCISCO IS PREPARED TO LEAVE THE CITY, FOR THE BELIEF IS FIRM THAT SAN FRANCISCO WILL BE TOTALLY DESTROYED.

DOWNTOWN EVERYTHING IS RUIN. NOT A BUSINESS HOUSE STANDS. THEATRES ARE CRUMBLED INTO HEAPS. FACTORIES AND COMMISSION HOUSES LIE SMOULDERING ON THEIR FORMER SITES. ALL OF THE NEWSPAPER PLANTS HAVE BEEN RENDERED USELESS, THE "CALL" AND THE "EXAMINER" BUILDINGS, EXCLUDING THE "CALL'S" EDITORIAL ROOMS ON STEVENSON STREET BEING ENTIRELY DESTROYED.

IT IS ESTIMATED THAT THE LOSS IN SAN FRANCISCO WILL REACH FROM $150,000,000 TO $200,000,000. THESE FIGURES ARE IN THE ROUGH AND NOTHING CAN BE TOLD UNTIL

A view up Market Street from the Ferry Building. Street car service was restored within days of the fire.

Streets, at the end of Buchanan, was known as Funston Playground for many years. (It was later renamed George R. Moscone Recreation Center to honor Mayor Moscone, slain on November 28, 1978.)

Funston was the hero not only of the earthquake and fire, but also of the monumental cleanup and rebuilding that followed. Hundreds of thousands of homeless had to be sheltered and fed. There were ninety-thousand refugees camped just in the Presidio, and twice that number spread around in other parts of the City. Relief trains loaded with food rolled into the Bay Area from all over the country. The Army sent every tent and all the spare rations it possessed, along with thousands of troops. By June, ten per cent of the U.S. Army was in San Francisco.

One month later they were gone. "The City That Knows How" seemed to rise from the ashes like the phoenix on the San Francisco city flag. The *Examiner* edition of Sunday, April 22, just four days after the earthquake, reported that street cars were running again on Market Street and boasted that the "Future is bright for San Francisco." A lot of people seemed to agree—in the ten days following the quake, 220 couples took out marriage licenses. As it had done six times in the 1850s the City prepared to re-build. It was a point of pride among residents that when they began clean-up operations, the bricks were still almost too hot to touch.

More than 5,000 wooden shacks ("earthquake cottages") were hastily constructed, and by the time the Fall rains arrived, all of the homeless had moved out of tents and into more solid shelter. "Camp Richmond," where many of the cottages were built, stretched from Eleventh Avenue to Fifteenth Avenue, from Lake Street all the way south to Cabrillo. Less than a year after the earthquake, on March 3, 1907, the mayor proclaimed Cleaning Day, when the last of the debris had been removed. In June 1908, the only refugee camp remaining in the City was dismantled, and within three years after the disaster, all but 8,000 of the 28,000 destroyed buildings had been replaced. Life had returned to normal.

The earthquake, and its aftermath, provided material for countless City legends. The story is told of a piano that had somehow escaped the flames when it was abandoned in the street by a fleeing refugee. Another resident, it is said, walked up to the keyboard and tapped out a song as the fire raged all around him. The song he played was "There'll Be A Hot Time In The Old Town Tonight."

Enrico Caruso also figured prominently in many a tall tale from the earthquake. The world's greatest tenor fled the City, via a ferry to Oakland, and a train to New York. When he arrived there, newspaper reporters asked him for his reaction to the earthquake. He is supposed to have said, "Give me my old Vesuvius!"

More reliable is the testimony of photographer Arnold Genthe, who saw Caruso sitting on the front steps of the St. Francis Hotel early Wednesday morning. The opera star, obviously dazed, was dressed only in a fur coat and pajamas, and could be heard muttering to himself, "'Ell of a place. 'Ell of a place. I never come back here." He never did.

The Flood Mansion and the Fairmont Hotel on Nob Hill. The News *edition of April 18 reported* "Thousands who went to bed wealthy last night awoke this morning practically penniless."

While walking around the City today, it is still possible to see evidence of the cataclysm that occurred nearly ninety years ago. The row of Victorian houses on Guerrero Street, between Clinton Park and Duboce Street, was saved by the Army dynamite teams, who halted the fire at that point, just before it spread uphill on Market into the Castro district. About thirty-four of the City's earthquake cottages still exist today, some having been incorporated as add-ons to private homes. Most are to be found in the Richmond district, though a few are in the hills above Dolores Park.

Walking south on Dolores Street from the Mission, you are following the fire line. Everything on your left was destroyed in 1906 and rebuilt afterwards. To your right, some buildings survive from before the earthquake. **If you walk up to the edge of the park at Twentieth Street and go right one block to Church Street** you can see the fire hydrant that miraculously continued to function after the quake. Every year a ceremony is held to give the hydrant a fresh coat of gold paint in appreciation of the role it played in saving the Mission.

If you are in San Francisco on April 18, you can join the few remaining survivors of the quake (and their many nostalgic supporters), who meet at Lotta's Fountain annually at 5:12 A.M. This reunion has been a City tradition since 1924. The Fire Department Museum usually provides an old "hand-pumper" fire engine for the occasion, and the local press gives the event adoring coverage. At Market and New Montgomery the Sheraton Palace Hotel occupies the site of Ralston's Palace, and while it is not quite on the same scale as its predecessor, it is still, well, palatial. The central courtyard where elegant carriages used to make their entrance is now a restaurant serving delicacies like Quail Ralston and "Palace Silver Dollars" (scallops with truffles).

A little farther out Market Street, between Fourth and Fifth, the inner facade around the front door of the Emporium is all that remains of the original building. Even that would have been blasted to oblivion, but the director of the San Francisco Mint stopped cleanup crews from using dynamite there. He was worried that the explosions might damage the Mint building around the corner at Fifth and Mission. When the new Emporium was built, designers incorporated the old facade into their plans.

Nob Hill lost most of the mansions that once graced its summit. The Fairmont Hotel, under construction in 1906, was badly damaged but was rebuilt. James Flood's mansion was likewise gutted, but the brownstone shell survived and, after some remodeling, now houses the Pacific Union Club. The other great buildings, constructed of wood, were completely destroyed. The Mark Hopkins Institute of Art (formerly Mark Hopkins' home, on the site of the Mark Hopkins Hotel) and the Stanford mansion next door burned in the early morning hours Thursday. A short time later the homes of Charles Crocker and his son William H. Crocker, which occupied the block where Grace Cathedral stands today, joined the expensive pyre. All that remained of the A. N. Towne mansion, which stood on the site of the Masonic Auditorium, was a marble archway. It was moved to Golden Gate Park near Lloyd Lake on Kennedy Drive, and is now

Ralston's Palace Hotel, 1906

The Sheraton Palace Hotel today

known as, "The Portals of the Past."

Lillie Hitchcock Coit came back to San Francisco from Paris in 1923. The former gadfly of genteel City society was nearly eighty years old, but the wild escapades of her youth were still San Francisco legends: the cockfights, the cigars, the bourbon straight up, the all-night poker games. Lillie symbolized the Old City and a glorious past that was long gone. She noted that the old Palace Hotel, where she had once staged a boxing match in her rooms, was no more. Lillie told her friend, author Gertrude Atherton, "San Francisco is no longer a wild place. Like me, it has settled down."

In a sense she was right. The new City was not just rebuilt, it was refounded, and some of the element of fantasy was missing. The great wooden mansions on Nob Hill, part Bavarian castle and part cuckoo clock, were replaced by apartment houses and hotels, sensibly done up in brick and concrete. And San Francisco business leaders rebuilt the downtown area prudently, with Ionic columns and other neo-classical touches for the conservative banking and financial institutions.

The whimsical flavor that had once defined San Francisco was never really lost. San Franciscans have always recognized the value of their unique history; indeed, they frequently bemoan the fact that the present, no matter how wonderful, can never measure up to the mythic times gone by. When the 1909 Commission met, to rename hundreds of City streets, they made a deliberate effort to preserve the cultural richness that is San Francisco's heritage. Their work guaranteed that the history of the old City would live on, if only in the street names.

Other clues are also there for the careful detective. The following section of this book offers five walks that will show you the evidence of the past that can still be seen in many areas of the City.

STREET WALKS

to some of the City's most interesting historical sites

WALK #1

The first walk starts at the Ferry Building and proceeds up Market Street, Geary Street, and Maiden Lane to Union Square. The route is almost completely flat and covers about twelve blocks.

San Francisco has always been a maritime city. Until the 1930s, when the Golden Gate Bridge and the Oakland-Bay Bridge were built, nearly everything came and went by ship. At the height of the ferryboat era, 50 million people passed through the Ferry Building annually. It was the busiest passenger terminal in the world except for Charing Cross Station in London.

Construction of the building you see today began in 1896. Before that, passengers used a much more modest building that resembled a barn. Amelia Ransome Neville, in *The Fantastic City*, wrote that the old building

> *was a long brown shed facing a plank-paved plaza, not at all an entrance to impress arriving visitors . . . The new Ferry Building finally rose in place of the shed, its tall, slender tower, copied from the Giralda of the Cathedral in Seville, dominating this foyer of the City.*

The clock in the Ferry Building tower stopped at 5:12 A.M., on April 18, 1906, when the earthquake struck. The tower itself was damaged, but was later repaired. In the Loma-Prieta earthquake of 1989 (the "World Series Quake") the clock also stopped; City residents hope it will continue to run uninterrupted for a long time to come.

The clock in the Ferry building tower.

Walk across the Embarcadero to the foot of Market Street. On your right, you can see Vaillancourt Fountain, as you cross Justin Herman Plaza. The fountain is the work of Canadian sculptor Armand Vaillancourt, and has been the source of much controversy. People seem to have very strong opinions about it. San Francisco *Chronicle* architecture critic Allan Temko, for instance, called it "several tons of almost incredibly ugly, brutal, pretentiously simple-minded and literally insipid concrete." But many other people like it, so decide for yourself.

Continuing straight ahead, keep to the right-hand side of Market Street. Spear Street and the Federal Reserve Bank building will be across Market on your left. On your right is California Street and the end of the cable car line. Cable car tickets and information are available at the booth just to the right of the tracks. (At this writing, one-way tickets cost $2; for $6 you can buy a pass that's good for one day of unlimited rides on all Muni vehicles.)

Continue southwest on Market, passing Beale Street and Fremont Street on your left. Where Bush Street runs into Market is a statue "dedicated to mechanics by James Mervyn Donahue in memory of his father Peter Donahue." In the 1850s Peter Donahue (with his brothers, James and Michael) expanded a small blacksmith shop into San Francisco's first foundry, the Union Iron Works. They produced stamp mills that crushed ore for the Comstock silver mines, manufactured steam locomotives, and later ventured into boat building.

One more block takes you to First Street, which really was the "first street" before landfilling began in Yerba Buena Cove. A plaque set in the sidewalk on the southwestern corner of First and Market marks the old shoreline. A second plaque, near the Donahue monument, also indicates where the original Cove began.

Continue southwest on Market. A certain amount of zigging and zagging is required to stay in the pedestrian crosswalks where Market crosses Battery and Sansome streets. This is because Jasper O'Farrell laid out Market Street on an angle to the rest of the streets. Notice also how wide Market is (one-hundred-and-twenty feet); this extra width is what got O'Farrell in so much trouble with San Francisco property owners (see Chapter 3).

Where Montgomery and Market intersect, you are at the site of George Hyde's property. It's difficult to believe looking at the urban congestion all around you now, but when Hyde built his house here in 1848, his friends all wondered why anyone would choose to live so far "out of town." On your right, a granite column with two brass sculptures celebrates the admission of California to the Union in 1850, and has a quotation from W. H. Seward: "The unity of our empire hangs on the decision of this day."

On the next block is a fountain donated to San Francisco, by Lotta Crabtree (1847-1924). The Lola Montez protégé had the cast-iron column and fountain installed in 1875 in gratitude to the city where she got her start. Lotta became a star at age eight, performing in gold mining camps, and was at one point the highest-paid performer in America.

An inscription on the column also commemorates a Christmas Eve, 1910, performance by Luisa Tetrazzini (the opera star of voracious appetite for whom Turkey Tetrazzini was created). San Francisco, at the time, was competing with New Orleans to be the site of the proposed Panama-Pacific International Exposition. The night Luisa Tetrazzini sang, the weather was perfect, and news reports of the performance influenced Exposition authorities to choose San Francisco. Some 250,000 people crowded into the area around Lotta's Fountain that night. Ms. Tetrazzini's lucid soprano notes hung in the windless evening air, and opera aficionados enjoyed an experience they would long remember. Amelia Ransome Neville said of the event:

> Those who heard her said her silver
> voice seemed to rise to the stars through
> the still night; and the utter silence of the
> great crowd in the dark streets was
> curiously thrilling.

Bearing right on Geary, you will be able to see some palm trees three blocks ahead. They are in Union Square, our destination, but we are going to take a slightly less direct route. Turn right on Kearny, go half a block, and turn left on Maiden Lane. Formerly named Morton Street, this was once the center of San Francisco's "red light district." Many people will tell you that the name was changed in an effort to clean up the City's image. This

Lotta Crabtree's Fountain, around 1915

makes a good story, but is not really how the name change came about. After the fire of 1906, Morton Street was renamed Union Square Avenue. In 1910, the name was changed again, to Manilla Avenue (continuing the theme of the Dewey Monument in Union Square.) Sometime later, a nearby jeweler named Albert Samuels asked that the name be changed yet again, to Maiden Lane. Maiden Lane was a street in the jewelry center in New York City, and Samuels thought it would lend some class to the neighborhood to use the same name. And that's how a street formerly lined with bordellos came to be called Maiden Lane.

Looking toward Union Square from Maiden Lane, the City Christmas tree is visible during the winter holidays. The first City tree was erected under orders from Norton the First, Emperor of the United States and Defender of Mexico. This charming crackpot was a San Francisco fixture in the 1850s, 60s, and 70s. He began life as Joshua Norton, but after losing his money and his sanity in an attempt to corner the rice market in 1853, he was reincarnated as Emperor Norton. He appeared on San Francisco streets wearing his own version of imperial military uniform: a jacket bedecked with gold braid, large gold epaulets, and a splash of colorful ribbons across his chest. A high beaver hat with long ostrich feathers completed the whimsical improvisation.

The Emperor cut quite a figure as he walked around San Francisco with his two mongrel dogs, Bummer and Lazarus, tagging along behind. City residents not only humored him, they cherished him; his royal edicts revealed a goodness of heart that outweighed any infirmity of mind. He frequently wrote the Kaiser, the Czar, Queen Victoria, and Abraham

Norton I, Emperor of the United States and Defender of Mexico

Union Square as it appears today

Lincoln with helpful suggestions on how the planet might be better governed. He ordered (and the City approved) that a lighted Christmas tree be erected in Union Square for the enjoyment of San Francisco's children.

Emperor Norton printed his own money, which San Francisco merchants obediently honored. The Central Pacific Railroad allowed him free transportation and dining car service on its trains. The California state legislature reserved him a seat in the Senate gallery, where, with Bummer and Lazarus, he often observed the proceedings. And when the Emperor's original uniform became threadbare, the City passed an ordinance that granted him thirty dollars per year to purchase new garments befitting his regal status. When Emperor Norton died in January 1880, twenty thousand mourners turned out for the funeral.

If you are visiting San Francisco in the Christmas season, your view looking up Maiden Lane will be of the tree At other times of the year, the view will be of the Dewey Monument. This tall column was constructed "to commemorate the victory of the American Navy under George Dewey at Manilla Bay May First, 1898."

You are now in Union Square, donated by John White Geary and named for the speeches and rallies held here in support of national unity in the 1850s and 1860s.

You are also in the heart of San Francisco's shopping area. You can board the Powell Street cable car line here, in front of the Saint Francis Hotel, on the west side of the Square.

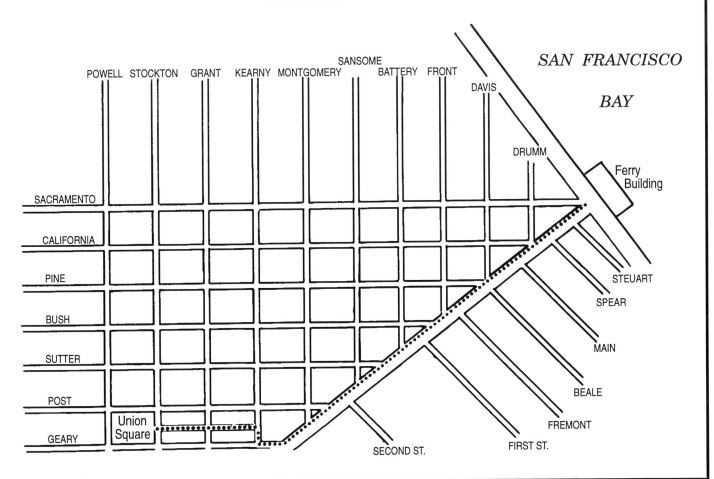

WALK #1

SAN FRANCISCO

BAY

POWELL STOCKTON GRANT KEARNY MONTGOMERY SANSOME BATTERY FRONT

DAVIS

DRUMM

Ferry Building

SACRAMENTO

CALIFORNIA

PINE

BUSH

SUTTER

POST

GEARY

Union Square

STEUART

SPEAR

MAIN

BEALE

FREMONT

FIRST ST.

SECOND ST.

Walk #2

This walk will take you to the top of Telegraph Hill. Though the route is only seven or eight blocks long, it is very steep, and is recommended only for energetic walkers. (Others can take the 39 Coit bus to see Coit Tower and the view from the top.)

Most visitors to San Francisco soon find their way to North Beach to enjoy the fine restaurants and coffee houses and to take in the ambience of the City's old Italian district. **This walk starts at the corner of Filbert Street and Columbus Avenue. If you walk east on Filbert, Washington Square park will be on your right.** This park, like Union Square, was donated to the City by Mayor John White Geary when he returned to his native Pennsylvania in 1852. It was a disreputable place, used as a dumping grounds (and later as a graveyard), until Columbus Avenue was cut through the existing grid of City streets in 1872-1873. By then the graves had been moved, some greenery was planted, and a white picket fence ran around the perimeter.

The water fountain in the park, with the statue of Benjamin Franklin, has an interesting story behind it. It was installed in 1904, having been given to the City some years earlier by a Dr. Henry Cogswell. The good doctor was a teetotaler, and his plan had been to construct at least one water fountain for every hundred bars in San Francisco. Even at those favorable odds, however, Cogswell was hopelessly outnumbered, and he gave up long before he had finished the task.

Continue east on Filbert Street, which climbs with increasing steepness as it nears Coit Tower, the 170-foot-high fluted granite monument in front of you. After you cross Grant Avenue, the sidewalk has stairs cut into it; by the time you reach Kearny Street, the sidewalk-with-stairs becomes stairs-without-sidewalk. But don't give up. In the Chamber of Commerce Handbook for San Francisco (1914), Frank Morton Todd wrote:

The counterpart of Telegraph Hill exists in no other large city in the United States. No one can begin to know San Francisco until he has climbed it.

Historically, the hill has played an important role. It takes its name from a semaphore station, called the Inner Signal Station, that was established on the summit in 1849. From that vantage point, spotters could see ships approaching the Golden Gate. Information about the ships was relayed to observers downtown through a system of semaphore signals. Merchants would then know what type of ship to expect and its probable cargo, information that was of great value in the competitive business world. The flags used to signal were not always visible because of fog, and in 1853 an electric telegraph was installed. The *Annals*

Telegraph Hill from Stockton and California streets, 1856.

reported that the proprietors of the telegraph, Sweeny and Baugh,

have also established in Sacramento Street, near Montgomery, a Merchants' Exchange . . . in the spacious rooms of which are always to be found the latest papers from all parts of the world. These enterprises have proved exceedingly lucrative to their projectors.

One famous story concerns the hand signals that had originally been used to notify businessmen of incoming ships. Practically everyone in San Francisco knew these signals by heart, and could tell if the arriving ship was, say, a cargo vessel from Hawaii, or the mail boat. It seems that one night during a very amateur production of Shakespearean drama, the over-emoting actor on stage spread his arms wide and delivered the line, "What means this, my lord?" At which point a heckler in the back row bellowed, "Sidewheel steamer!"

As you gasp your way up the final flights of stairs, you can take comfort in knowing that you have climbed the *easy* side of Telegraph Hill. (The Filbert Street steps you have just ascended also continue down the east side.) The eastern slope of the hill is a lot steeper due to quarrying that was conducted there for many years. Some of the sandstone and shale that make up the hill was used as ballast in the old sailing ships, and was ultimately discarded in foreign ports. (Parts of Telegraph Hill can now be found as far away as China!) But, most of the thousands of cubic yards of material that were removed are much closer to home, in the landfill and seawall along the Embarcadero. Two brothers named George and Harry Gray enthusiastically engaged themselves in that project until the time of World War I. In their twenty years of blasting, they ignored several court orders to cease and desist, and only determined neighborhood opposition saved Telegraph Hill from complete destruction.

The last block or so of your walk, along the sidewalk on the right-hand side of the road, takes you to the base of Coit Tower, named for Lillie Hitchcock Coit. Lillie arrived in San Francisco, in May 1851, at age eight, at the time of the City's worst fire. This seems appropriate: although Lillie Hitchcock was engaged to be married numerous times (she eventually did marry wealthy mining investor Howard Coit), her greatest love was always for the firefighters of San Francisco. Lillie was forever rushing off to help the firemen at the first sound of the alarm. On one occasion she even left a wedding rehearsal and fought the fire while wearing a formal bridesmaid's outfit.

The adoring crew at Knickerbocker Engine Company #5 awarded Lillie honorary membership and adopted her as the company mascot. For the rest of her long life she faithfully observed their anniversary, every October 17, and always signed her name "Lillie Hitchcock Coit—#5." She had a gold "#5" lapel pin fashioned for her, wore it day and night, and ultimately was buried wearing it. Lillie even, it was whispered, had "#5" embroidered on her underwear.

Chasing fire engines was considered unladylike by most

Lillie Hitchcock Coit in her firefighting youth.

Coit Tower

of City society, which was scandalized by her behavior. But Lillie seemed to welcome scandal, a penchant she may have inherited. Lillie's mother was a southern belle who found herself unable to pay the property taxes on the Carolina plantation she had inherited from her parents. So, prior to moving to San Francisco, she burned the place down.

Clearly, Lillie had something of the same wild nature. She bleached her brown hair a shocking blonde, dressed in men's clothing to attend cockfights, drank bourbon expertly, and was known as a pretty good poker player. Moreover, she was immune to the tut-tutting of San Francisco's more genteel society, having inherited upon Howard Coit's death a fortune of which most of her detractors could only dream.

Lillie travelled widely, to Hawaii and to Paris, where she translated Civil War reports for Napoleon III and acted as foreign correspondent for the San Francisco *Evening Bulletin*. When she returned, she settled into a suite at the Palace Hotel. On one occasion she staged a middleweight, boxing match in her rooms there—which created quite a sensation. Newspapers from as far away as New York and Boston reported the event.

Even greater notoriety followed. In November 1903, Lillie was entertaining a gentleman friend, one J. W. McClung, in her sitting room at the Palace. In burst Alexander Garnett, a distant relative of Lillie's. It is not known exactly what happened next, but Garnett shot and killed McClung. Lillie was traumatized. She moved to Paris and lived there for nearly twenty years, refusing to return until Garnett's death in 1923.

Lillie then came back to San Francisco and took up residence at the St. Francis Hotel, where she stayed until her death in the summer of 1929. She bequeathed $125,000, "for the purpose of adding beauty to the City which I have always loved." The funds were used to build Coit Tower and to erect a small statue in Washington Square.

It is widely (and erroneously) believed that Coit Tower was designed to resemble a firehose nozzle of Lillie's day. Don't believe it, but do go see the tower, which commands sweeping views of the City and the Bay. The ground floor houses frescoes which were completed in 1934, painted as a Public Works of Art project during the Great Depression. For a small fee you can ride the elevator to the top and enjoy the panorama.

WALK #2

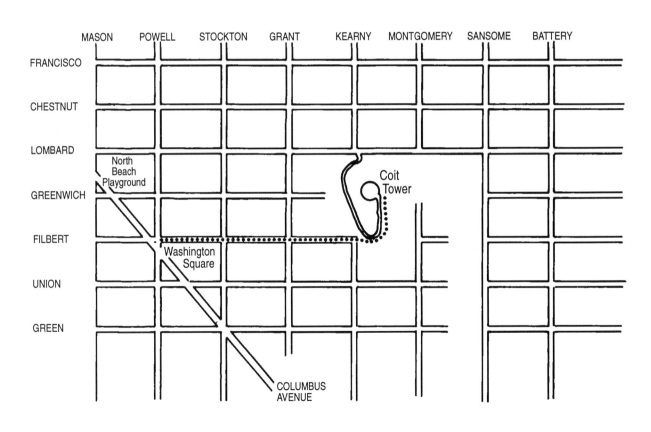

MASON POWELL STOCKTON GRANT KEARNY MONTGOMERY SANSOME BATTERY

FRANCISCO

CHESTNUT

LOMBARD

North
Beach
Playground

GREENWICH

Coit
Tower

FILBERT

Washington
Square

UNION

GREEN

COLUMBUS
AVENUE

WALK #3

This walk retraces the steps of Captain John B. Montgomery and his men from the *Portsmouth*, who raised the American flag at Yerba Buena's central plaza (now called Portsmouth Square), on July 9, 1846. **The walk is short, about six blocks, and is level except for the last block.**

It is difficult to determine exactly where Montgomery and his men landed when they came ashore to claim Yerba Buena for the United States. Before the Cove was filled in, Broadway ended somewhere between Montgomery and Sansome, and the small wharf, built by William Squire Clark, extended into the Bay from there. While the *Portsmouth* rode at anchor in the Cove, a party of about seventy men came ashore near Clark's Point in the ship's boats. A Petty Officer from the group, Joseph Downey, wrote a series of reminiscences for a weekly literary magazine called, *The Golden Era*, in the 1850s. Downey says only that they played Yankee Doodle as they "trudged proudly up through Montgomery Street to Clay, up Clay to the Plaza." **This walk will begin (somewhat arbitrarily) at Battery and Jackson, go the two blocks up Jackson to Montgomery, and from there rejoin with more certainty the steps of the *Portsmouth*'s crew.**

Starting at the southwest corner of Jackson and Battery, keep to the south (left) side of Jackson and walk west. Somewhere near here are buried the remains of the brig *Euphemia*, which Mayor John White Geary bought to serve as San Francisco's first City Jail. The *Euphemia*, like hundreds of other ships, had been abandoned in the Cove when her crew ran off to the gold fields. A few of the ships were hauled up onto shore and used as shops, warehouses, and even hotels, but for most of them Yerba Buena Cove would be their final anchorage. They were stripped of any useful fittings, scuttled, and covered over with sand taken from the City's hills.

Walking west on Jackson Street, you are in the oldest surviving neighborhood in San Francisco, one of the few areas within the fire zone that was spared in 1906. On both sides of the street are brick buildings that date from the Gold Rush. Today they are occupied mainly by antique stores, interior decorators, and art galleries. Number 415 Jackson was, for nearly forty years (1857-1894), the location of the Ghirardelli Chocolate Factory and Offices. Domingo Ghirardelli arrived from South America, in 1849, and set up shop on Battery Street serving a Gold Rush clientele. He moved a number of times before settling in at the Jackson Street address. Soon after the Chocolate King retired in 1892, his sons transferred the operation to its present location near Fisherman's Wharf.

On your right a small alley named Balance Street connects Jackson to another alley, Gold Street. Balance Street is named not for the scales that were used to weigh gold, as you might assume, but for an abandoned ship of that name which lies somewhere beneath your feet. Take a minute to explore these two byways before returning to

Jackson Street. Brick buildings all around you show the marvelous craftsmanship and style of the Gold Rush period. Number 472 Jackson Street is a particularly fine example, built in 1851.

Across the street from that building, Hotaling Street runs into Jackson. The three-story Hotaling building on the corner (at 429 Jackson) was once a liquor warehouse, in fact the largest on the West Coast. It escaped destruction in 1906 through the heroic efforts of a Navy Lieutenant named Frederick Newton and his men. They ran a hose all the way from Pier 43, over Telegraph Hill, and down to Jackson Square. Salt water from their ship's pumps enabled them to stop the fire's spread into this area. The survival of the warehouse inspired Charles Field to write a famous doggerel:

If, as they say, God spanked the town for being over frisky,
Why did He burn the churches down and save Hotaling's whisky?

The view south on Hotaling Street is a remarkable study in contrasts. Directly ahead is the Transamerica Pyramid, one of the City's most modern skyscrapers; on both sides of Hotaling are cobblestone and brick buildings that are among the City's oldest.

Continue west on Jackson Street another half-block to Montgomery, and go left. You are now on what was (and still is) San Francisco's version of Wall Street. From the earliest days, banking and investment houses could be found along Montgomery Street. On the northeast corner

Hotaling's whiskey warehouse

of Jackson and Montgomery stood a branch of the St. Louis-based Lucas, Turner & Co. A brass plaque on the wall marks the location. This bank was managed in the mid-1850s, by William Tecumseh Sherman, who had come to California as an aide to Military Governor Richard Mason, in 1847. Sherman would later achieve fame (or infamy) for his devastating march through Georgia in the Civil War.

As you turn onto Montgomery, you are near where Sam Brannan began the Gold Rush. On May 12, 1848, he marched down the street waving a whiskey bottle full of gold dust and shouting, "Gold! Gold on the American River!" Within a few weeks San Francisco was deserted, as every dreamer who could walk or limp headed for the hills.

A number of plaques along Montgomery commemorate historic places and events. One at 722 Montgomery "marks the birthplace of Freemasonry in California October 17, 1849." This building and the annex to the right of it at number 728 are owned by famed trial lawyer Melvin Belli. (Belli's law offices are located nearby, on the corner of Montgomery and Pacific.) Originally a warehouse, 722 Montgomery was later a theater, and at one time hosted performances by singer/dancer Lotta Crabtree. Number 728, next door, was also a warehouse, but had apartments upstairs. French artist, Jules Tavernier, while on his way home from a tour of the South Seas, lived for a time in one of the apartments. Oscar Wilde visited him here during his famous 1882 lecture tour. Wilde didn't fit-in very well in San Francisco. He was in the habit of wearing black velvet knee-breeches, white silk shirts, a green velvet vest, and black silk stockings while addressing his audiences. According to

Amelia Ransome Neville, San Franciscans never did grasp the finer points of Aestheticism, and for his part Wilde "was frightfully bored, and looked upon California as a sort of No Man's Land where he spoke to penguins."

Bret Harte also lived at Number 728 while he was writing, "The Luck of Roaring Camp." Bret Harte and Mark Twain both sold stories to the *Golden Era* while they were in San Francisco. (Harte left town in 1872, Twain a few years before.) Harte didn't have to go far to hand in his manuscripts: the office of the *Golden Era* was right next door, at number 732.

The next block is Washington Street, where Columbus Avenue joins Montgomery Street at a sharp angle. The rectangular grid of City streets, established by Jasper O'Farrell's 1847 survey, did not take into account the steepness of San Francisco's hills when it was laid out. Columbus Avenue is at an angle to the other streets because it was cut through the existing grid in 1872-1873, following the route of the old footpath from the Cove to the Presidio. That footpath sensibly kept to the flatlands between Russian Hill and Telegraph Hill. Columbus Avenue is thus one of the few concessions made to the topography of the City. The rest of the streets charge straight up and down the steepest parts of San Francisco without the slightest concern for geological realities. Some climb and descend at angles of more than thirty degrees, and, as you will quickly find out if you do much walking, sidewalks built in the form of stairs are common.

The old and the new —Transamerica Pyramid and buildings that date from the Gold Rush.

The **Transamerica Pyramid on your left occupies the block where Columbus Avenue meets Montgomery Street,** a historic location. In 1853 Henry Halleck constructed an office building known as the Montgomery Block on this site. Halleck had been a delegate to the state Constitutional Convention in Monterey a few years before, and would later serve as Chief of Staff for the Union Army in the Civil War. When he proposed the neo-classical four-story building, City residents scoffed at its enormous height and called it "Halleck's Folly." The brown stucco structure was the tallest building west of the Mississippi River at the time. Many famous local artists and writers lived in the apartments upstairs, while professional offices occupied the ground floor. It was in one of these offices that James King of William died after being shot by James Casey, in 1856.

The Montgomery Block (known irreverently by locals as "The Monkey Block") also housed part of the rare book collection that former mayor, Adolph Sutro, had bequeathed to the City at the turn-of-the-century. Sutro, a Prussian-born engineer, made his fortune by building a tunnel in the Comstock Silver Mines, in Nevada. This was not just any tunnel. Sutro's idea was to dig up into the mine at an angle from the hillside below, boring a shaft more than 20,000 feet long. The tunnel, it was hoped, would drain water from the mines and provide ventilation for the workers. Intense heat, at the depths where the richest deposits were located, had been an enormous problem for the miners. Ice was lowered to one of the chambers below ground to provide a cool rest area, but in the Comstock Lode nearly one hundred pounds of ice per man were being used every day. It was almost as much work to provide the ice as to dig the mine.

Sutro's tunnel just might be the answer.

After nine years of labor, the tunnel at last connected with the mine works, 1,650 feet below ground, in the summer of 1878. By that time the mine was already deeper than the tunnel. No ore was ever hauled out through it, nor were the mines noticeably cooler for the effort. Nevertheless, it did provide drainage for huge quantities of groundwater, and Sutro was able to sell his share in the project for nearly a million dollars, just before the silver in the Comstock Lode ran out. Sutro retired to San Francisco to live the good life of real estate speculator and philanthropist.

At both endeavors he was extraordinarily successful. Adolph Sutro had an uncanny knack for buying property that other people considered worthless, then developing it successfully. At one point he owned one-twelfth of all the real estate in San Francisco, including what is now called Sutro Heights, Parnassus Heights, and Point Lobos, at Seal Rocks. There he built the world's largest indoor swimming pool complex (Sutro Baths), and the fabulous "Gingerbread Palace" Cliff House next to the baths. The public was enchanted with the wonderland Sutro had created at San Francisco's western-most point, and in 1894 elected him mayor on the Populist ticket.

When he died in August 1898, he left his library to the City. It was probably the finest private collection in America, almost 250,000 items housed in three different locations around town. The Montgomery Block held much of the treasure, and as the 1906 fire advanced towards that building, the Sutro Collection was loaded onto wagons and moved to the Mechanics' Pavilion for safekeeping. But in a particularly ironic twist of fate, the Pavilion building and most of the priceless Collection were destroyed, while the Montgomery Block survived intact.

In 1959, during a period of civic improvement, the Montgomery Block succumbed to the wrecker's ball, and in 1972 the Transamerica Pyramid rose in its place. A kind of tradition was preserved for the site: at forty-eight stories— 853 feet including its spire—the Transamerica building is the tallest in San Francisco today.

Continue south one more block and cross to the southeast corner of Clay and Montgomery. A brass plaque on the wall commemorates Captain Montgomery's landing. **For the last two blocks you have been following the old shoreline of Yerba Buena Cove.**

As you stand facing west up Clay Street, everything behind you, including most of the Financial District, sits on landfill. Now look to your left across Montgomery Street. The Tokai Bank, in the light-gray skyscraper, that fills the half-block from Commercial to Sacramento, is on the site of a wood-frame building put up by merchant, Jacob Leese, in 1838. The lot between Commercial and Clay, where the Bank of Canton now stands, is where the Hudson's Bay Company did business from 1841 to 1845. William Howard and his partner, Henry Mellus, bought the building when the English firm left San Francisco, and the two went on to become the City's leading businessmen. In those days their property fronted on Yerba Buena Cove; now the Bay waters are seven blocks away.

1856 view of Portsmouth Square at the intersection of Washington and Kearny streets.

Portsmouth Square as it appears today.

127

Cross Montgomery Street and walk up Clay Street the final block to Portsmouth Square. The brick building at 669 Clay, on the left, was built in 1867, and now houses a bar/restaurant and an accounting firm. Number 661, next door, also dates from the nineteenth century, but the other brick buildings on this block were built after the 1906 earthquake.

Across the street several brass plaques commemorate the Pony Express, which was established by Russell, Majors, and Waddell, in April 1860. The operation was short-lived, lasting just over a year, but the mystique and romance of the lone riders galloping across the wild west live on. The trip from St. Joseph, Missouri, to Sacramento, California, took ten to twelve days (half as long as by stagecoach). A record run was once accomplished in seven days and seventeen hours, to carry Lincoln's inaugural address to California. The invention of the telegraph spelled the end of the Pony Express, but not of the romantic legend.

In Portsmouth Square you are surrounded by the early history of San Francisco. The Holiday Inn on the east side of the Plaza is on the lot where Sam Brannan and his colony of Mormons camped after they disembarked from the *Brooklyn* in 1846. Just a block away, at 743 Washington Street, Brannan published Yerba Buena's first newspaper, the *California Star*. Near the center of the Plaza a small monument marks the location of the flagpole where Montgomery had raised the Stars and Stripes a few weeks before Brannan's arrival. Nearby, a granite and bronze sculpture remembers writer Robert Louis Stevenson, who lived for a time at 608 Bush Street. When Stevenson sailed off to Samoa in 1888 he chartered his sailboat through a firm with offices in the Montgomery Block.

Portsmouth Square occupies the four lots that were left open for a public plaza, in the Vioget Survey of 1839, when the little settlement on the shores of the Bay covered all of eight blocks. The Plaza was the town center, the social and political hub for Yerba Buena, and later San Francisco. The first Customs House and Hall of Justice were here. Here, the First Committee of Vigilance hanged John Jenkins; it was in Portsmouth Square that thirty-thousand people gathered to hear Edward Baker deliver the eulogy for David Broderick in 1859; and Mayor Schmitz met here with the Committee of Fifty on the morning of April 18, 1906, as the fires that would destroy San Francisco were gaining momentum. So much has changed since then. Portsmouth Square was renovated in 1993, and is now a popular place for the City's Chinese community to stroll about, play card games, and socialize. But sometimes, when the wind is right, you might be able to hear a lost echo of Yankee Doodle from Montgomery's band, "consisting of one drum and fife, with an occasional put-in from a stray dog . . . in the line of march."

WALK #3

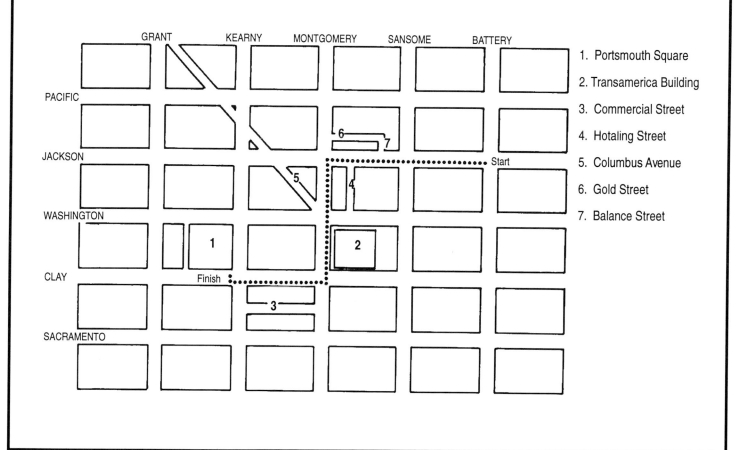

GRANT KEARNY MONTGOMERY SANSOME BATTERY

PACIFIC

JACKSON

WASHINGTON

CLAY

SACRAMENTO

Start

Finish

6

7

5

4

1

2

3

1. Portsmouth Square

2. Transamerica Building

3. Commercial Street

4. Hotaling Street

5. Columbus Avenue

6. Gold Street

7. Balance Street

Walk #4

This walk takes you around the top of Nob Hill, showing where the great nineteenth century mansions stood before the 1906 earthquake. The walk begins with a cable car ride up California Street. You can board the cable car anywhere along the route where you see a brown-and-white "Cable Car Stop" sign. I recommend starting at the eastern (Market Street) end of California Street, where there is a booth for tickets and information. You can buy a one-way ticket for $2.00, or an all-day pass for $6.00, that entitles you to unlimited rides on any of the Muni system's cable cars, buses, and trolleys. Energetic walkers should ride the cable car up as far as Powell Street. If you are not comfortable walking up steep hills, remain on board for one more block and get off at Mason Street, where you will rejoin the walk on its flatter sections.

What we call Nob Hill today was formerly known as the "Clay Street Hill," or the "California Street Hill", and for a long time was considered almost uninhabitable. It was a great place to go for a family picnic or to enjoy the view, but the daily drudgery of hauling water and firewood up the hill was more than most people were willing to undertake. The best residential area in the City was then on Rincon Hill, in a neighborhood known as South Park.

What turned Nob Hill into the *ne plus ultra* residential district was the invention of the cable car by Andrew Hallidie. A cherished City legend has it that one day the London-born Scottish engineer was watching a team of horses trying to haul an overloaded wagon up a steep hill. One of the horses slipped on the cobblestones, dragging the entire team backwards down the hill. Out of compassion for the poor beasts, Hallidie conceived the idea of streetcars powered by underground cables.

It was natural that Andrew Hallidie would think of an invention that involved steel cable. He held numerous patents on the cable-operated machinery that was used in the Comstock mines in Nevada. There the hoisting works and stamp mills relied on what was called "wire rope," actually a flat, woven tape about five or six inches wide and three-quarters of an inch thick. By 1870, A.J. Hallidie & Company were manufacturing several kinds of wire rope in a factory at Mason and Chestnut streets. Demand in the mines had fallen off, but since the cables used by the cable cars were expected to last only twenty months, replacing them would help keep Hallidie & Company profitably employed for the forseeable future.

In August 1873, when the first cable car line opened on the six blocks of Clay Street between Kearny and Jones, the public was amazed. Transportation without horses, without steam! The cable cars were a sensation, and by 1880 there were eight lines operating in the City on one-hundred-and-twelve miles of track. As you ride up California Street to the start of our walk, you will undoubtedly experience the excitement that San Franciscans felt in 1873. The cable cars

Looking up Powell Street at the summit of Nob Hill.

utterly delightful. Today, only about seventeen miles of the system survive, but the cars are protected as America's only mobile National Landmark. They will continue to operate regardless of cost as San Francisco's least-sensible and best-loved form of transportation.

The California Street Hill, made accessible by Hallidie's brainchild, immediately became the fashionable address for San Francisco's plutocrats. People started calling it "Nob Hill." The name probably comes from "Nabob" (a potentate in the Mogul empire), though "snob," "hobnob," and even "knob" also have their supporters. The top of the hill commanded sweeping vistas of the entire City. Just as importantly, the entire City would have to look up at the sprawling mansions and, one assumed, be suitably impressed.

Richard Tobin, the founder of Hibernia Bank, was one early settler. He set the pace for the millionaires who followed by indulging in vast quantities of marble and mahogany, and building an observation tower fifty feet high. During parties, guests could watch fireworks displays staged for their enjoyment down on the Bay.

Tobin's brother-in-law and partner, James Ben Ali Haggin, owned an entire block on the northern shoulder of Nob Hill, bounded by Taylor, Mason, Washington, and Jackson. His passion was horses: the stables behind the four-story, sixty-room house comfortably accommodated forty horses and eighteen carriages. But Tobin and Haggin, though wealthy by the standards of mere mortals, were not really in the same league with the Silver Barons and railroad tycoons who were later to occupy the summit of San Francisco's Mount Olympus.

Our walk begins at the corner of California Street and Powell, where you should get off the cable car and walk south on the right hand side of Powell. (To avoid the steep portions of this walk, stay on the cable car for one more block and get off at Mason Street.) You will be following a row of urban "lollipop" trees and a high, dark stone wall on your right, the original retaining wall for the Stanford mansion. Leland Stanford, with his partners Collis Huntington, Charles Crocker, and Mark Hopkins, had made his fortune building the Central Pacific Railroad. Stanford's retaining wall was constructed by railroad laborers, who used the same Rocklin Quarry stone that the Central Pacific used in its bridges and tunnels. Though Stanford was the first to build a Nob Hill mansion (in 1876), the rest of the "Big Four" would soon follow, each trying to outdo the others in ostentatious expenditure.

The house itself was located where the Stanford Court Hotel now stands. Amelia Ransome Neville likened it to "a great gloomy barn." As barns go, this one must have been rather comfortable, if its $2,000,000 price tag is any indication. There was an art gallery, an elaborate master suite, and a central rotunda that rose three stories to a glass roof. The exterior of the house was highly-flammable redwood painted dark brown. When the fire swept over the top of Nob Hill in 1906, the Stanford mansion burned (in Neville's words) "like any shanty."

Go right (west) on Pine Street. There is a large stone

The Big Four: (clockwise from upper left) Mark Hopkins, Collis P. Huntington, Charles Crocker, Leland Stanford. At center is Theodore Judah, the engineering genius who designed the Central Pacific Railroad.

tower with a brass finial on top of the wall on your right about half-way up the block. This vaguely Moorish tower marked the property boundary between Stanford and his neighbor, Mark Hopkins.

When you get up to the corner of Pine Street and Mason, you are at the entrance to Hopkins' home. Where you see the automobile entrance, next to the "One Nob Hill Circle" sign, enormous oak doors used to allow carriages to ascend an "S"-shaped driveway up to the house.

Hopkins may have had the most impressive of all the "Big Four" mansions. It was a castle, built of wood and painted to look like stone, on a scale any feudal lord would envy. The gray towers were illuminated at night and could be seen from many miles south of the City. Hopkins himself never lived there, in fact took little interest in the place as it was being built. He was happy to putter around in his vegetable garden behind the simple home he lived in down the hill. Mark Hopkins just wrote the checks, and his wife, Mary, directed the construction. He gave her *carte blanche*, letting her indulge a passion for fanciful ornamentation that drove several designers to despair. Intricate mosaics, enormous murals, inlaid hardwoods, and lavish furnishings clashed in a wild hodge-podge of styles that could charitably be called "eclectic," with a price tag of around three million dollars.

Mark Hopkins died in 1878, before the house was finished. Soon afterwards Mary went East, where she built another house, on a comparable scale, in Great Barrington. She married her young architect, who inherited the Nob Hill

When money is no object: the Stanford mansion (right) and the Mark Hopkins castle.

mansion when she died. He, in turn, donated the house to the San Francisco Art Institute in February 1893. It burned in 1906, and twenty years later a hotel genius, named George Smith, opened the Mark Hopkins Hotel on the site. The Top of the Mark bar, which Smith created, remains one of the City's favorites.

Turn right on Mason and climb the steep hill back up to California Street. Cross California, noticing the distinctive ringing of the cable in the slot, and turn left, crossing Mason Street. (This is where you will rejoin the walk if you opted to remain on the cable car at Powell Street.) The handsome brownstone on your right was originally the home of James Flood, and was the only mansion on Nob Hill to survive the fire. The interior was gutted, of course, but the exterior walls withstood the inferno without serious damage. Some minor remodeling was done by famed architect Willis Polk, who added the rounded wings on the east and west sides, but today the house is essentially unchanged from when James Flood occupied its forty rooms. (The Flood mansion is now privately owned by the Pacific Union Club, and is not open to the public.)

Flood and his friend, William O'Brien, had been partners in the Auction Lunch, a Montgomery Street restaurant popular with San Francisco stockbrokers. While serving up their famous fish stew to the lunch crowd, the two Irishmen couldn't help overhearing insider secrets about mining companies. In an era when the flimsiest rumor could send a stock soaring (or plummeting), Flood and O'Brien listened carefully, acted cautiously, and rode the winners. One stock

The Silver Barons, or "Little Four" as they were sometimes called: (clockwise from upper left) John W. MacKay, James Flood, William S. O'Brien, and James G. Flair.

135

in particular, Hale and Norcross, rose from $41 to $7100 per share in one year. The two restaurateurs had served their last bowl of chowder.

Flood and O'Brien joined forces with two friends, John W. MacKay and James Fair, who had been modestly successful miners in Nevada. The four made a strange but effective team. Fair was something of a master mechanic, the nuts-and-bolts man. MacKay was probably the most knowledgeable about mining. Flood knew the financial markets, how to buy up stock quietly and cheaply. O'Brien had no particular talents, but he was an immensely likeable sort, and he came along for the ride because he was Flood's friend. Flood would later explain his loyalty by saying simply, "I would never have anything that Billy didn't share." For his part, O'Brien confessed, "I just got hold of the tail of a kite and hung onto it."

With their stock market earnings the four men bought a mine in Nevada called the Consolidated Virginia. MacKay somehow had the intuitive genius to keep digging where others before him had abandoned the claim, and a few hundred feet further down tapped into the richest silver vein ever discovered. The Big Bonanza, as it came to be called, yielded three hundred million dollars worth of silver in six years, roughly a million dollars a month for each of the Bonanza Kings.

The brownstone mansion you see today was Flood's effort at conspicuous consumption. Flood had already experienced the joys of piling stone upon stone when he built Linden Towers, a forty-five room spread on the peninsula in Menlo Park. For five years, hundreds of workmen labored to complete the sprawling palace. It featured a rosewood master suite, eleven guest suites, a forty-foot-long dining room table, and solid silver door-knobs. But Flood didn't like the place, especially when neighbors began calling it "Flood's Wedding Cake." After just a few years in the house, during which time Hallidie's cable cars had made San Francisco's higher elevations accessible, Flood moved to Nob Hill and began building again.

The sandstone for the exterior walls was brought from Connecticut, in imitation of the New York brownstones that were then the rage among the Morgans, Carnegies, and Rockefellers in that city. There was a kind of competition between the *nouveau riche* on the east and west coasts of America at the time. The easterners, having been ridiculed by European Old Money for years, comforted themselves by laughing at the westerners. Californians, it had to be grudgingly admitted, were every bit as *riche* as their eastern counterparts, but at least they were slightly more *nouveau*, and thus more worthy of derision. New Yorkers delighted in telling the story of a copy of the Venus de Milo that the French government had donated to San Francisco's Art Association. Supposedly, the Association had complained to Wells Fargo that the statue was missing its arms when it was delivered. And, the story continued, Wells Fargo paid up without complaint, lest the public should learn of its carelessness.

As you walk past the Flood mansion, heading west on California Street, notice the weathered, beautifully-wrought brass fence that runs along three sides of the

The Flood mansion, with James Flood's $30,000 fence in the foreground.

property. James Flood paid $30,000 dollars for this fence, and employed a servant whose only job was to keep it shining. For years this anonymous servant polished his life away, moving slowly around and around the block. As you can tell by the heavy patina on the fence now, it has gone unpolished since the poor fellow retired.

One more block along the walk takes you to the corner of Taylor and California streets. On your left is the Huntington Hotel. On your right is Huntington Park, on the site of the house Collis P. Huntington bought from his business associate, David Colton. Colton's house was also laughingly called a "wedding cake," and was probably more deserving of the name than Linden Towers. Painted white, the two-story mansion covered most of the block. Six Ionic columns graced the entryway on the California Street side, and elaborate classical friezes protruded above each of the tall, narrow windows. The ornamentation appeared to be less the work of an architect than of a confectioner, like something piped on with a pastry bag. Still, it was a grand house, copied from an Italian *palazzo*, and entirely worthy of the man who was chief legal counsel for the most powerful railroad in America. The Big Four may have found it somewhat conservative, however, judging by their efforts to outdo it with their own homes.

Charles Crocker, in particular, took a more determinedly lavish approach. Technically speaking, the home he built in 1877 was in the Deuxieme Empire Italian villa style, but that description doesn't do justice to the elaborate, $2.3 million pile that occupied the block across Taylor Street from Colton's more modest lodgings. Forests were leveled and quarries depleted in an effort to satisfy the quest for more. A phantasmagoria of corbels, arches, columns, gables, and towers exhausted the imaginations of designers and confounded the skills of an army of craftsmen. When it was completed, the Crocker mansion's exterior made a statement of luxurious excess unlike any other. Willis Polk examined the house with his expert eye and pronounced it "the delirium of a wood carver." Inside, more than a million dollars' worth of paintings (including Millet's, *The Sower*) kept the acres of interior walls from becoming monotonous. For the library, decorators ordered books by the yard, buying whatever was needed to fill the available shelves, with little regard for titles or authors.

In 1888, Charles Crocker built another house, a relatively simple Queen Anne style mansion, on the southwest corner of the property, and gave it to his son as a wedding present. Father and son would probably have been very happy together on Nob Hill if it weren't for the irritation of a certain neighbor. An undertaker named Nicholas Yung had been living on a tiny parcel of land near the corner of Sacramento and Taylor since before the advent of the cable car. Charles Crocker, who already owned the rest of the block, offered to buy Yung's property, but he refused to sell. Crocker was enraged, and directed his carpenters to construct a forty-foot-high wooden fence (the "Spite Fence") around three sides of Yung's house. Still Yung refused to sell, and he spent many years living at what must have seemed like the dreary bottom of a four-story elevator shaft.

The battle was not all one-sided, however. Apparently the undertaker exacted his own form of revenge on Crocker.

One legend recounts that Yung built an enormous coffin with a skull and crossbones on the lid, and stood it on the roof of his house where Crocker would see it every day as a reminder of his mortality.

Cross Taylor Street and turn right. The new stairway leading to the main entrance of Grace Cathedral will be on your left. After the 1906 fire, the Crocker family donated the entire block bounded by California, Jones, Sacramento, and Taylor to the Episcopal Church, and the cornerstone for Grace Cathedral was laid on January 24, 1910. (Coincidentally, this was the sixty-second anniversary of the discovery of gold at Sutter's Mill.) When the new stairway was constructed in the summer and fall of 1993, a fence along the sidewalk was carefully removed and saved. It is all that remains of the Crocker mansion that once stood on this site.

Walk up the stairs to the cathedral entrance. The enormous bronze doors in front of you are a copy of the baptistery doors in Florence designed by Lorenzo Ghiberti in the Fifteenth Century. Known as the "Gates of Paradise" doors, they depict biblical scenes in ten beautifully sculpted panels. **If you walk to your right, around to the north side of the cathedral facing the new fountain,** you can see the surviving section of the Crocker fence in its new location.

Retrace your path back down the cathedral steps, turn left, and walk up to Sacramento Street. Just before you get to the corner (where there is a low wall built of Rocklin Quarry stone) look down at the sidewalk on your left. You will see some letters cast in the concrete,

Grace Cathedral

including the date 1871. This was the date of the manufacturer's patent for the "ASP," or "artificial stone pavement." The concrete was poured in the late 1870s, and may well be the oldest sidewalk in the City.

Walk left up Sacramento Street as far as the entrance to the courtyard between Grace Cathedral and the New Chapter House. You are now at what was the main entrance to the Crocker family compound. In the last decades of the nineteenth century, luxurious carriages would enter here to deposit their wealthy passengers at Charles Crocker's door.

If you examine the sidewalk here, you will see that the old concrete ends and a modern slab begins, just about where a large stone column forms part of the wall around the church's property. There is a row of granite stones at this transition point, set in the sidewalk concrete at right angles to the curb. These stones mark one boundary of the lot where Nicholas Yung's house once stood. **Now do an about-face and walk back down towards Taylor Street, keeping an eye on the sidewalk. Fifteen paces downhill you will see another row of granite stones which mark the other property line.** Nothing else remains to recall the "spite fence," the undertaker's home, or the coffin on the roof.

Cross Taylor Street and continue walking east on Sacramento Street. Huntington Park, the site of "Colton's Wedding Cake," will be on your right, containing a small playground and fountain. **You will cross a narrow lane, Cushman Street, which separates the park from the grounds of the old Flood mansion.**

There is a magnificent brass gate with lions' heads and fancy scrollwork on the northwest corner of the grounds, part of James Flood's $30,000 fence. **Continue east, following the fence to Mason Street, and turn right.** A second, identical, brass gate, facing Mason Street, was at the other end of James Flood's curving driveway.

The Fairmont Hotel will be across Mason Street on your left. James Fair had intended to build a palace that would be even more lavish than the mansions of the other Nob Hill nabobs. He bought the block bounded by Mason,

The Fairmont Hotel today.

California, Powell, and Sacramento, and began planning how to outshine Mark Hopkins and Leland Stanford, across the street. It is interesting to imagine what Fair would have come up with, but unfortunately he died after only a granite retaining wall had been constructed.

Fair's daughters, Virginia and Tessie, inherited the property and built the Fairmont Hotel there. The hotel was nearly finished at the time of the 1906 fire. Though the outer stone shell of the building survived, the structural steel skeleton was damaged by the intense heat and had to be replaced.

When you get back to the corner of California and Mason, go left and walk down the hill one bock to Powell Street. From here there are several options: A.- You can board the cable car to Fisherman's Wharf on the Powell & Hyde Street line, or B.- take the California Street line back to our starting point on Market Street. Also, C.- Union Square is an easy four-block walk away, downhill on Powell Street.

While you are considering your decision, notice how the cable car lines cross at Powell and California. The cable cars are propelled by reaching down through a slot in the street with a clamping device that grabs onto the moving cable. In the cable car barn at Mason and Washington streets, electric motors keep the continuous loops of cable for the three lines running at a constant speed (nine-and-a-half miles per hour). To move forward, the gripman on board the car pulls a lever to grab the cable; to stop, he lets go of the cable and pulls another lever to actuate the brakes.

You might be wondering how the lines can cross without the clamping mechanism of the car on one line getting snarled on the cable for the other. The answer is that the gripman has to be paying close attention to his job. The cable on the Powell & Hyde Street line is lower than the California Street cable. When the car comes up Powell Street from Pine, the gripman must let go of the cable (known as "the rope") so that he will clear the California Street cable. His forward momentum then carries him across California Street, where he stops to let passengers on and off. To complete the journey to Fisherman's Wharf, he continues coasting down the hill, using only the brakes, all the way to Jackson Street. There the gripman pulls on the lever to re-engage the cable, and the car sets off once again at its stately nine-and-a-half miles per hour.

If you look at the street pavement at the intersection of Powell and California, you will see the gripman's instructions written in yellow paint on the asphalt. In one direction it says "Take Rope," and in the other, "Let Go."

Countless tourists have marveled at the cable cars, but perhaps none has expressed his astonishment as well as Rudyard Kipling did in 1889. Then twenty-four years old and just back from India, and he wrote that

San Francisco is a mad city, inhabited for the most part by perfectly insane people whose women are of a remarkable beauty.

The cable cars, Kipling continued, seemed nothing less than magical:

> *There is no visible agency of their flight . . . I gave up asking questions. If it pleases Providence to make a car run up and down a slit in the ground for many miles, and if for two pence-half penny I can ride in that car, why shall I seek the reasons of the miracle? They turn corners almost at right angles, cross other lines, and, for all I know, may run up the sides of houses.*

The fare is now somewhat higher than the "two pence-half penny" it was in Kipling's day, but the cable cars have lost none of their magic.

Where the cables cross at Powell and California.

WALK #4

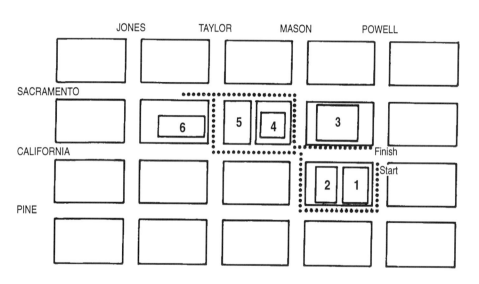

JONES TAYLOR MASON POWELL

SACRAMENTO

6 5 4 3

CALIFORNIA

Finish

2 1 Start

PINE

1. Stanford Court Hotel

2. Mark Hopkins Hotel

3. Fairmont Hotel

4. Pacific Union Club

5. Huntington Park

6. Grace Cathedral

WALK #5

This walk explores the Fisherman's Wharf area. We will start at the famous "Fisherman's Wharf of San Francisco" sign at Taylor and Jefferson streets, go west three blocks to the Cannery, then walk along Aquatic Park to the National Maritime Museum and Ghirardelli Square.

Loneliness will not be a problem for you on this walk. Regardless of what time of day (or year) you go to Fisherman's Wharf, you are sure to have the company of large numbers of tourists. The area ranks right at the top of the list of things that visitors want to see in the City, along with the cable cars and the Golden Gate Bridge. But don't be put off by the crowds. A stroll along the waterfront, with its spacious views of Alcatraz, Angel Island, and the Bay, is still a wonderfully enjoyable experience.

Development in this area of San Francisco is nothing new. The northern edge of Yerba Buena Cove originally ended at Clark's Point. From there the City's "North Beach" ran along the narrow strip of land, between Telegraph Hill and the Bay, ending at North Point, about where the intersection of North Point Street and Grant Avenue is now. The shoreline then followed a curving course along another cove until it came to Black Point, a promontory due west of North Point near present-day Fort Mason.

As early as 1850, land speculators were betting that San Francisco would grow in this direction. A City alderman, Henry Meiggs, actively pushed the idea along, building a road around the eastern edge of Telegraph Hill, filling in tidelands, and constructing a 1,600-foot-long wharf. Meiggs Wharf stuck out into the Bay from Powell Street (which then ended around Francisco), and Redwood Coast lumber schooners unloaded logs there from the Mendocino coastal forests. A lumber mill at Mason and Francisco streets sawed timbers and planks for the rapidly-growing City.

All was going well for Henry Meiggs until the economic downturn of the mid-1850s, when investment money for the scheme dried up. But since Meiggs was an alderman, it was easy for him to get his hands on municipal warrants, and he used them to continue financing his development. He forged some of the warrants; others had been signed, blank, by the mayor, and Meiggs simply filled in the amounts as needed.

"Honest Harry" Meiggs sailed out through the Golden Gate for South America in October 1854, when his shenanigans came to light, leaving nearly a million dollars of bogus paper in his wake. Ironically, he was a huge success building mountain railroads in Peru. The six-hundred-mile run he built from Lima to Huancayo, an engineering marvel of hair-raising zigzags, bridges and tunnels, is the world's highest single-gauge rail line, and is still in use today. But even the millions of dollars that Meiggs made in South America weren't enough to buy a return ticket to respectability in San Francisco, and he never did come back.

Meiggs' Wharf was in some ways a forerunner of today's Fisherman's Wharf, a combination dock, bar, restaurant and amusement park. Where the wharf met land, a saloon keeper, named Abe Warner, ran a weird establishment known as the "Cobweb Palace." Patrons imbibed in a milieu of tropical parrots, half-wild monkeys, and spider's webs that the superstitious Warner never cleared away. Another business, a kind of carnival/museum, had an "educated pig" that would play cards with customers. There was even a seafood restaurant that provided wooden mallets to use on the all-you-can-eat crab legs that came free with the purchase of a nickel beer.

But Meiggs' Wharf was not Fisherman's Wharf. San Francisco's fishermen were concentrated along North Beach in the wharves at the end of Green, Union, and Filbert streets. What had begun as a handful of Italian fishermen in the 1850s, had by the mid-1880s become the Italian Fishermen's Association, a powerful union in control of a major industry. Something like 50,000 pounds of fish were being sold daily in San Francisco, and the immigrants themselves were adding a welcome dash of Mediterranean color to the City. At dockside in "Italy Harbor" (as it was called) wives mended nets, young boys dexterously packed them into the cramped net lockers, and mustachioed *paterfamilias* in billowy white shirts and brightly colored waist sashes presided over the operation.

In 1885, the City established docking facilities for two hundred-sixty-five fishing boats at the Filbert Street Wharf. Most of the boats were *feluccas*, small double-enders with a shallow draft and triangular, lateen-rig sails. They proved perfectly suited to duty on the Bay and in the waters outside the Golden Gate, able to withstand strong winds and swift currents in spite of their small size and minimal freeboard. Even with the introduction of steam power in 1885 and gasoline engines twenty years later, the sail- and oar-powered *felucca* remained a fixture on the Bay until after the first World War. Crabbing was the most common occupation (the catch as early as 1887 amounted to an incredible 300,000 crabs), though salmon and bottom fish were also taken.

At the end of 1900, the City, under orders from the state Fish and Game Commission, moved the *pescatori* to the present site of Fisherman's Wharf. They weren't happy about it. The new location offered little shelter from the winds and currents coming through the Golden Gate. It wasn't until 1926 that Pier 45 and the Hyde Street Pier were completed, which provided some measure of protection.

As we start our walk from Taylor and Jefferson streets, some of the flavor from the old days may still be apparent. Charm has a way of being lost in the packaging process, and fast food joints and T-shirt shops have all but crowded out the local fishermen, but some of the place names recall old glories. Many of the restaurants in this area were started by Italian fishermen who got their start selling fish door-to-door from a basket.

Begin the walk by going west on Jefferson Street, keeping to the right-hand side of the street. Tarantino's, the first restaurant you will pass, was founded by the family of Gaetano Tarantino, who arrived in San Francisco in 1883.

A few steps further along you will come to the basin where the few remaining working boats tie up. On the pier across the inlet you will see Fisherman's Grotto #9. This was the first two-story restaurant at the Wharf, built in 1935 by long-time fisherman, Mike Geraldi. On the right is Alioto's, founded by Nunzio Alioto, in 1925.

Just to the left is another restaurant, Sabella and La Torre. Antone Sabella opened the place in 1920, and followed with a larger venture in 1939 to cater to the crowds that came for the World's Fair on Treasure Island.

Continue walking west. Across the street to your left will be the Guinness Book of World Records Museum and a long row of T-shirt and souvenir shops.

At Jones Street, there used to be four spaces provided by the City where boats could be hauled out for maintenance and repairs. They were located just about where Castagnola's restaurant is now, on your right. Tomaso Castagnola opened the Wharf's first restaurant in 1915, and the Panama Pacific International Exposition in that year helped make the eatery a success. It was Castagnola who popularized crabmeat cocktail. Prices have risen astronomically since those days, but *Cancer Magister* (Dungeness crab) is still cooked in steaming outdoor vats and served along the Wharf. Just past Castagnola's you will walk through an arcade that has several businesses selling the walk-away delicacy.

The next block after Jones is Leavenworth Street. A one-block extension of Leavenworth north of Jefferson

Boats in the basin at Fisherman's Wharf.

has been renamed Richard Henry Dana Way, in honor of the author of *Two Years Before the Mast*. Dana sailed out of San Francisco Bay in December, 1835, making a famous prediction: "If California ever becomes a prosperous country, this bay will be the center of its prosperity."

Dana Way connects to Fish Alley, the working part of Fisherman's Wharf that few visitors see. Take a moment to explore the alley and you may even see a real fisherman, though it's more likely you will see a truck driver bringing in fish from other parts of the West Coast. Bay Area fisheries have been depleted by many years of overfishing and pollution. Dungeness crab is no longer found in the Bay; sardines disappeared in the 1950s. Fisherman have tried to adapt, modifying their equipment to fish for herring on their annual Bay spawning run, for example, and moving operations to Alaskan waters for part of the year. But the economics of fishing are probably more difficult now than at any time in the past.

Another block west takes us to The Cannery, the large brick complex on your left. These two buildings have had a varied history since their construction in 1907. Originally they were the home of a packing plant for the California Fruit Canners Association. Starting in 1909, the eighteen canning companies that made up the consortium used the Del Monte label, and by 1916 they were canning more peaches than any other operation on earth. The plant was shut down during the Great Depression, and for the next twenty years the buildings went through a number of tenants. The U.S. Post Office used them as a warehouse, and for a time they were occupied by the British Motor Car Company. Both buildings were nearly torn down to make way for something more modern, but a far-sighted investor named Leonard Martin bought them in 1963. After five years of upgrading and remodeling, the retail complex opened, with shops spread over three levels. You may be able to catch a show on the stage in the central courtyard. Jugglers, clowns, and other street artists perform here frequently, and some of them are remarkably talented.

The Hyde Street Pier across Jefferson Street from the Cannery is a State Historic Park run by the National Park Service, and with a nominal fee is one of the best deals at Fisherman's Wharf. Seniors and children are free. On the first Tuesday of each month, admission is free for everyone. You can board three ships, the *C. A. Thayer*, the *Eureka*, and the *Balclutha* for self-guided tours. Ranger-guided groups are also organized daily. Check with the rangers for times.

The *C. A. Thayer* entered service as a three-masted, lumber schooner in 1895. Starting in 1912 she made annual trips bringing men and supplies to Bristol Bay, Alaska, and returning with barreled salmon. From 1925 to 1950 she was used in the Bering Sea as a codfisher, the last commercial sailing ship to operate on the West Coast. On board are numerous artifacts from the days of "iron men and wooden ships." Photographs and explanatory plaques convey what life at sea was like, from the Victorian elegance of the captain's cabin to the monastic simplicity of the crew's accomodations in the fo'c'sle.

The *Balclutha* is truly a San Francisco ship. Built in

View of the Hyde Street Pier and the Balclutha.

Scotland in 1886, she made the City her home port for forty-five years. Five times she rounded Cape Horn (the sailors called that frozen and forbidding place "Cape Stiff,"), hauling California wheat to Europe and returning with Newcastle coal, but she spent most of her working life bringing canned salmon down from Alaska. Below decks there is an interesting scale model of a salmon packing plant of the era, and old 100-pound fish boxes are piled in the hold as they would have been on the return run to San Francisco. After the *Balclutha* was retired from commercial service, she appeared as one of the square-riggers in *Mutiny on the Bounty* (the 1935 version with Charles Laughton and Clark Gable.) As on the *C. A. Thayer*, lots of period furnishings and fittings recall bygone days.

The *Eureka*, berthed across the pier from the two sailing ships, is a steam-powered paddlewheeler that was used as a ferry on San Francisco Bay for more than sixty-five years. Originally named the *Ukiah*, she hauled both railroad cars and passengers. The U.S. government used her to carry freight cars full of munitions in World War I, and overloaded her so badly that the hull had to be completely rebuilt. Only the keel and four frames could be saved, but after reconstruction the *Eureka* was the largest wooden passenger ferry ever built.

In 1920, the reincarnated and renamed ship was put back to work as an automobile and passenger ferry between Sausalito and the City, docking at the Hyde Street Pier that is now her final resting place. The Pier in those days was officially designated as part of State Route 101, the Redwood Highway. People driving north along the coast put their cars on the ferry, crossed to Sausalito, and continued the drive from there, technically without ever leaving Route 101. The opening of the Golden Gate Bridge in May 1937, alas, put an end to the Hyde Street Pier's "freeway" status.

Nautical buffs should inquire about tours of the ship's boiler room to see the impressive, four-story steam engine, and car fanciers will love the antique autos on the lower deck. Before leaving the Hyde Street Pier, be sure to look for the *feluccas* (modern replicas, not originals) that can be seen near the end of the pier. There are also other attractions: a Polynesian canoe, the Bay's last scow schooner (the *Alma*), and a boatwright's shop that gives demonstrations of traditional techniques.

Leaving the Hyde Street Pier, walk west on Jefferson Street. On your right will be two private clubs, the South End Rowing Club (organized in 1873), and the Dolphin Club (established in 1877). Both clubs, which moved to their present locations in the 1930s, promote aquatic activities on the Bay. Many Dolphin Club members swim daily in the numbing waters of Aquatic Park, and there are annual Alcatraz and Golden Gate swims.

At the southwestern corner of the Dolphin Club you will see two large, ships' propellers on the ground. Diagonally across the small parking lot to the left is a wide asphalt path leading up towards three evergreen trees. Follow this path uphill along the grassy lawn of Aquatic Park. This area rests on landfill, much of it rubble that was cleaned up after the 1906 earthquake and fire. Somewhere beneath your feet are thirty-million bricks from the Palace Hotel. It seems fitting that they should end up here, for this is where the builder of the Palace Hotel also ended his days.

William Ralston, like Mark Twain, had worked on Mississippi riverboats from an early age. In 1849, when he was just twenty-three years old, he set off from New Orleans for the California gold fields. Initially he made it only as far as Panama, where he joined forces with two friends and started a steamship company transporting the Forty-Niners to California. It wasn't until 1854 that Ralston settled permanently in San Francisco. His ferries carried Sierra-bound miners and supplies up the Sacramento River, and silver and gold on the return trip to San Francisco. Shipping led naturally to banking, and Ralston prospered. When the Bank of California opened in 1864, with Ralston in command and much of the Comstock Lode silver in its vaults, it controlled more capital than any other bank in the state.

The Comstock mines, according to some estimates, eventually produced $400,000,000 worth of silver. Unfortunately, getting at the richest deposits overwhelmed the technology of the day. Cave-ins, flooding, and searing temperatures halted efforts at about the five hundred foot level. Mining companies were determined to extract the enormous riches that lay tantalizingly out of reach, and they borrowed heavily to acquire the newest machinery. Ralston's bank was happy to lend them money at a discount, and happier still to foreclose on the loans when the miners' efforts failed. Before long the Bank of California had a monopoly on the entire operation. When new techniques

William Ralston

allowed the mines to descend deeper, William Ralston rode the wave of silver that flowed out of the hills and into San Francisco.

He was a complex personality, a modest man who nevertheless dreamed and planned and achieved on a vast scale. Investors developing a farming community in the Central Valley once asked him if they could name their new town "Ralston," but the banker insisted that he didn't deserve such an honor. In recognition of Ralston's modesty, they named the town "Modesto" instead.

Ralston, for all his personal humility, was also possessed by grandiose visions. He did nothing on a small scale. The Bank of California headquarters, at California and Sansome streets, was the finest commercial building in the City. It was modeled on the library of Saint Mark's Cathedral in Venice, and had a blue sandstone exterior. Ralston's mansion in Belmont had eighty rooms; even the stables boasted rare hardwoods inlaid with mother-of-pearl. And the Palace Hotel that Ralston planned would be the biggest, most luxurious hotel in America. It would, in fact, be far too large for a city the size of San Francisco, but that didn't matter to Ralston. San Francisco would grow, he was sure, and when it did the Palace Hotel would be ready.

He never lived to see it finished. The complicated banking and mining empire that Ralston had so carefully put together began to unravel with dizzying speed. First the silver in his star performer, the Ophir Mine, ran out; then financial commitments to an intricate tangle of other investments left him overextended. Nervous depositors made a run on the Bank of California, and on August 26, 1875, the bank closed its doors.

The following day Ralston resigned as Chairman and walked down to the Neptune Baths, at the foot of Larkin Street, for his customary afternoon swim. He was found floating face-down a short time later. Some said he died of a stroke, others that it was suicide.

Happier times are recalled by the brass plaque set in a large stone on your right as you continue walking along the path towards the National Maritime Museum. The marker commemorates Captain Juan Manuel de Ayala and the *San Carlos*, the first ship to enter San Francisco Bay. Ayala spent forty-four days anchored off Angel Island late in the summer of 1775, and his pilot, José de Cañizares, made the first map of the Bay.

Just ahead on the right is the museum, in the low white building at the foot of Polk Street. There are a number of great exhibits here, and admission is free (a donation is requested). The museum has a large collection of scale ship models, everything from John B. Montgomery's man-o'-war *Portsmouth* to Jack London's ketch, the *Snark*. The clipper ship models upstairs are of particular interest. In the roughly sixty years from the Gold Rush to the opening of the Panama Canal, nearly 10,000 voyages were made around Cape Horn. Only twenty-six of those voyages were completed in less than one hundred days, and the clipper ships accounted for twenty-two of them. The *Flying Cloud,* the most famous of all the clippers, once sailed from New York to San Francisco in eighty-nine days, a record that stood for more than a century.

On the ground floor of the museum there is a large covered balcony overlooking the Municipal Pier. Here

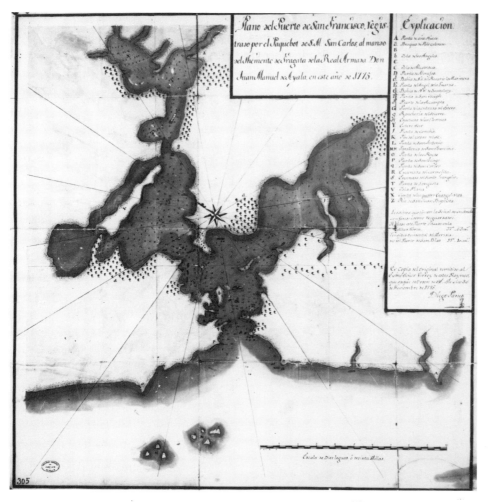

The first ship to enter San Francisco Bay was the San Carlos. Captain Juan De Ayala spent forty-four days anchored off Angel Island late in the summer of 1775, and his pilot, José de Cañizares, made the first map of the Bay.

you can see a display of actual mast sections from a square rigger and a schooner. The massive spars dwarf the nineteen-foot *Mermaid* next to them. In 1962, a young Japanese sailor made a three-month, solo voyage from Osaka to San Francisco aboard this tiny sloop, which he then donated to the museum.

Finally, the last stop on this walk is Ghirardelli Square. The sons of Italian chocolate maker Domenico (or "Domingo") Ghirardelli moved the business to this location in 1894, after the patriarch retired. The company had been based for many years at 415 Jackson Street (see Walk #3), and by that time was already a City institution.

Ghirardelli's now-legendary chocolate had arrived in San Francisco before he did. The confectioner was living in Lima, Peru, next door to a cabinetmaker named James Lick, and when Lick left for California aboard the brig *Lady Adams*, he brought six hundred pounds of the Italian's chocolate with him. (That the first Ghirardelli chocolate was brought to the City by a man named Lick, is a historical coincidence that can only be called "delicious"). In January 1848, North America had its first taste of Ghirardelli chocolate, and the reception was so favorable that James Lick convinced his former neighbor to relocate from Lima. Domingo Ghirardelli arrived the following year, and the rest, as they say, is history.

A labyrinth of shops now occupies the half-dozen buildings that make up Ghirardelli Square. Here you will find a wide variety of clothing stores, jewelry shops, art galleries, and gift shops. And if all this walking has whet your appetite, there are also fourteen restaurants you can choose from. May I suggest something chocolate for dessert?

WALK #5

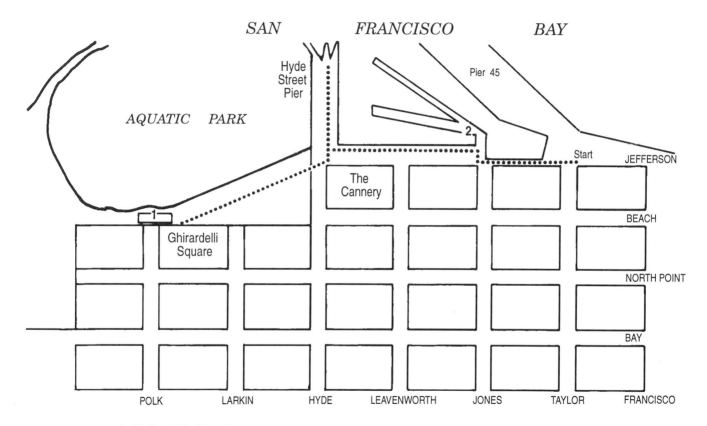

SAN   *FRANCISCO*   *BAY*

Hyde
Street
Pier

Pier 45

AQUATIC   *PARK*

2

Start

JEFFERSON

The
Cannery

BEACH

1

Ghirardelli
Square

NORTH POINT

BAY

POLK   LARKIN   HYDE   LEAVENWORTH   JONES   TAYLOR   FRANCISCO

1. National Maritime Museum

2. Fisherman's Wharf

APPENDIX ONE
Street Names

Strictly speaking, the San Francisco Board of Supervisors has the legal authority to approve all City street names. As a practical matter, however, the Public Works Department names streets that come into being from City-sponsored projects, and developers name new streets constructed in privately-funded subdivisions. Approval by the Board of Supervisors is nearly always automatic.

Some streets in San Francisco are named for those in other cities. Broadway, Greenwich Street and Lombard Street take their names from streets in New York, for instance. Sansome Street and Market Street are named for streets in Philadelphia.

The following streets are named for American Presidents: Grant Ave., Pierce St., Washington St., Lincoln Way, Fillmore St., Taylor St., Jackson St., and Polk St.

Many street names are of obvious origin: Maple Street, Cherry Street, Rose Street, etc. Note, however, that some pitfalls await the unwary: Pine Street and Bush Street were named for Isaac B. Pine and Dr. J. P. Bush. Even Main Street, contrary to what you might think, was named for a person, Charles Main.

The following list contains a brief selection of street names and their origins. Those marked with an asterisk are discussed in the text and can be found by referring to the index.

Alvarado St...........Juan Bautista Alvarado, Governor of Alta California 1836-1842
Annie St................Annie Russ, daughter of J. C. Christian Russ
Anza St.*...............Juan Bautista de Anza
Arguello Blvd.*....Don Luís Antonio Argüello
Baker St. *............Edward Dickenson Baker
Bartlett St.............Washington A. Bartlett
Battery St.*...........Named for a gun battery built at Clark's Point in 1846.

Beale St.*...............Edward F. Beale
Brannan St.*........Sam Brannan
Brenham Place*...Charles Brenham
Broderick Street*..David Broderick
Bryant Street*......Edwin Bryant
Bucareli Dr.*.........Lieutenant General Baylio Fray Don Antonio María Bucareli y Ursua
Buchanan St.........John C. Buchanan, one of Fremont's men who later served as an aide to alcaldes Edwin Bryant and George Hyde.

Bush St. ....Dr. J. P. Bush, an aide to Jasper O'Farrell.
Cabrillo St.* ....Juan Rodríguez Cabrillo
Castro St.* ....Named for a soldier in Anza's group, Joaquín Isidro de Castro, or perhaps for his descendant, José Castro.
Clay St.* ....Henry Clay
Cleveland St. ....Charles Cleveland, an early banker
Cole St. ....Cornelius Cole, a lawyer and publisher who was elected Congressman in 1863 and Senator in 1866.
Coleman St.* ....William T. Coleman
Crespi Drive* ....Father Juan Crespi
Davis St.* ....William Heath ("Kanaka Bill") Davis
De Haro St.* ....Francisco De Haro
Divisadero St. ......From the Spanish verb *divisar*, meaning "to see from a distance," not from the Spanish *dividir*, "to divide."
Drake St.* ....Sir Francis Drake
Drumm St.............Lieutenant Richard C. Drumm, who served in the Mexican-American War and the Civil War.
DuPont St.* ....Samuel F. DuPont, Captain of the *Congress* (now called Grant Ave.)
Eddy St. ....William M. Eddy, City Surveyor, later Surveyor General of California
Ellis St.* ....Alfred J. Ellis
Embarcadero ....Spanish word for "dock" or "pier."
Fell St. ....William Fell, a Danish-born Forty-Niner who became a popular merchant.
Folsom St.* ....Captain Joseph L. Folsom
Font Blvd.* ....Father Pedro Font
Franklin St. ....Benjamin Franklin, or perhaps for early merchant Selim Franklin.
Fremont St.* ....John C. Fremont
Funston Ave.* ......General Frederick Funston

Galvez Ave.* ....José de Gálvez
Geary St.* ....John White Geary
Gough St.* ....Charles Gough
Grant Ave.* ....Ulysses S. Grant
Green St.* ....Talbot Green, aka Paul Geddis
Guerrero St.* ....Francisco Guerrero, alcalde of Yerba Buena in 1836 and again in 1838-1839.
Haight St.* ....Henry Haight, lawyer, member of the Vigilance Committee, and California Governor (1867-1871).
Halleck St.* ....Henry Halleck
Harrison St. ....Edward H. Harrison, a member of the Stevenson Regiment of New York Volunteers, which arrived in California in 1847.
Hayes St. ....Col. Thomas Hayes, who owned a 160 acre parcel west of City Hall now known as Hayes Valley.
Hotaling St.* ....Anson P. Hotaling
Howard St.* ....William D. M. Howard
Hyde St.* ....George Hyde, alcalde from June 1847 to April 1848
Jackson St. ....Andrew Jackson
Jansen St.* ....Charles Jansen
Jessie St. ....Jessie Russ, daughter of J. C. Christian Russ
Jones St.* ....Elbert P. Jones, editor of the *Star* and owner of Portsmouth House, Yerba Buena's first hotel, near the corner of Clay and Kearny.
Judah St. ....Theodore D. Judah, who engineered the Central Pacific Railroad for the Big Four.
Junipero Serra Blvd.*

Father Junípero Serra

Kearny St.* .... Stephen Watts Kearny
King St.* .... Thomas Starr King
Laguna St. .... Named for Washerwoman's Lagoon, a small pond near Laguna and Greenwich streets.
Larkin St.* .... Thomas O. Larkin
Lawton St. .... Brig. General Henry W. Lawton, a hero of the Spanish-American War.
Leavenworth St.*

Thaddeus M. Leavenworth, a doctor, Episcopalian minister, and alcalde (from September 1848 to August 1849).

Leese St.* .... Jacob P. Leese
Leidesdorff St.* ..... William A. Leidesdorff
Lick Place* .... James Lick
Lyon St. .... Nathaniel Lyon, Captain of Troop C of the First Dragoons in 1848
Mason St. .... Richard B. Mason
McAllister St.* ...... Hall McAllister
McLaren Ave. ...... John McLaren
McCoppin St. .... Frank H. McCoppin, elected Mayor in 1867, State Senator in 1875.
Merritt St. * .... Ezekiel Merritt
Moncada Way ...... Captain Fernando de Rivera y Moncada
Montgomery St.* .. John B. Montgomery
Moraga St.* .... Lieutenant José Joaquín Moraga, of the Anza Expedition
Mulford Alley* ..... Prentice Mulford
Natoma St.* .... Named for a tribe of indigenous Californians who lived on the Feather River. The street was originally named Mellus St.
Noe St.* .... José de Jesús Noé, last Mexican alcalde and owner of a land grant that included most of San Francisco.

Noriega St. .... José de la Guerra y Noriega
Octavia St.* .... Octavia Gough
O'Farrell St.* .... Jasper O'Farrell
Ortega St.* .... Sergeant José Francisco de Ortega
Otis St. .... James Otis, elected Mayor in 1873, died in office in October 1875.
Pacheco St. .... Juan Salvio Pacheco, one of Anza's soldiers.
Page St .... Robert C. Page, a City clerk 1851-1856
Palou Ave.* .... Father Francisco Palou, Junípero Serra's close associate and biographer
Peralta Ave. .... Gabriel Peralta, a corporal in the Anza Expedition. The lands granted to him included most of Alameda, Oakland, and Berkeley.
Pico Ave.* .... Pío Pico, last Mexican governor of California
Polk St. .... President James Knox Polk
Post St. .... Gabriel B. Post, member of the 1849 Town Council (Ayuntamiento).
Powell St. .... Dr. William Powell, ship's surgeon on the *Warren*, a U.S. warship in the Mexican War
Ralston St.* .... William Ralston
Richardson Ave.*

William A. Richardson

Sanchez St. .... José Antonio Sánchez, commander of the Presidio and owner of a large land grant on the peninsula
Scott St. .... General Winfield Scott, Union Army commander in the Civil War
Sloat Blvd.* .... Commodore John D. Sloat
Steiner St. .... L. Steiner, who delivered water door-to-door in early San Francisco
Steuart St. .... William M. Steuart, aide to Commodore Thomas Ap Catesby Jones

Stockton St. .... Robert F. Stockton
Sutro Heights Ave.*
                    Adolph Sutro
Sutter Ave. .... John Sutter
Taraval St.* .... Named for an Indian guide to the Anza
                    Expedition
Truett St.* .... Miers F. Truett
Turk St. .... Frank Turk, an assistant to John White
                    Geary in San Francisco's first post office
Valencia St. .... Jose Manuel Valencia, one of Anza's
                    soldiers
Vallejo St.* .... General Mariano Guadalupe Vallejo
Van Ness Ave.* .... James Van Ness, Mayor in 1855-1856
Waller St. .... R. H. Waller, City Recorder in 1851
Webster St.* .... Daniel Webster

Photo List

Page VI   City of San Franciso Seal
Page VIII Talbot H. Green, Sam Brannan, Jacob P. Leese, Thomas O. Larkin, William D. M. Howard

CHAPTER ONE

Page 1   Sir Francis Drake
Page 2   Drake's "Plate of Brasse"
Page 4   Jose de Galvez
Page 6   Father Junipero Serra
Page 7   Don Gaspar de Portolá
Page 8   Alcatraz as seen from North Point, 1866

CHAPTER TWO

Page 9   Captain Juan Bautista de Anza
Page 12   Mission Dolores, 1870
Page 13   Missin Dolores and parish church
Page 16   Jacob P. Leese
Page 17   The Leese Family
Page 18   William D. M. Howard
Page 20   The 1839 Vioget map

CHAPTER THREE

Page 22   John C. Fremont
Page 24   Thomas O. Larkin
Page 25   Brass plaque of William A. Leidesdorff
Page 27   Don Mariano Guadalupe Vallejo

Page 28   California's state flag is modeled on the original Bear Flag
Page 30   Captain John B. Montgomery
Page 31   Washington Bartlett
Page 32   Typical sidewalk
Page 34   1847 O'Farrell Map of San Francisco
Page 34   Portion of 1849 William Eddy Map of San Francisco
Page 35   View of San Francisco in March 1847
Page 36   Old Saint Mary's Church, Chinese pagoda, Transamerica Pyramid
Page 37   General Pio Pico
Page 38   General Robert F. Stockton

CHAPTER FOUR

Page 41   Sam Brannan
Page 43   The *California Star*
Page 45   Colonel Richard B. Mason
Page 47   John Sutter
Page 50   Cable car on Hyde Street

CHAPTER FIVE

Page 52   State seal
Page 53   Henry Halleck
Page 57   John White Geary
Page 59   Devastation from the fire of May 4, 1851
Page 60   Devastation from the fire of June 22, 1851

Page 62   David C. Broderick
Page 63   Edward Baker
Page 64   Thomas Starr King and his wife
Page 65   Thomas Starr King

CHAPTER SIX
Page 68   Hall McAllister
Page 69   William Coleman
Page 71   Official Committee of Vigilance
          membership certificate
Page 74   James King of William
Page 75   Committe of Vigilance symbol
Page 76   Fort Gunnybags
Page 78   Cora and Casey hang at Fort
          Gunnybags

CHAPTER SEVEN
Page 82   Houses on Howard Street after the 1906
          earthquake
Page 83   Valencia Street Hotel
Page 85   General Frederick Funston
Page 87   Montgomery Block
Page 88   Group poses in front of the ruins of City
          Hall
Page 89   The ruins of City Hall
Page 90   Delmonico's Restaurant in 1906
Page 91   Dewey Monumenty in Union Square
          1906
Page 91   Dewey Monument in Union Square today
Page 92   Smoke from the Great Fire

Page 93   A horse-drawn fire engine
Page 96   Where the fire stopped, a view from
          Dolores Park
Page 98   Devastation from the 1906 earthquake and
          fire that followed
Page 99   More devastation from the 1906
          earthquake and fire that followed
Page 100 Headline from *The Call—Chronicle—
          Examiner* April 19, 1906
Page 101 View up Market Street from the Ferry
          Building, 1906
Page 103 The Flood mansion and Fairmont Hotel
          on Nob Hill
Page 105 Ralston's Palace Hotel, 1906
Page 106 The Sheraton Palace Hotel today

CHAPTER EIGHT
WALK ONE
Page 109 Clock in the Ferry building tower
Page 111 Lotta Crabtree's Fountain, around 1915
Page 112 Norton I, Emperor of the United States
          and Defender of Mexico
Page 113 Union Square as it appears today

WALK TWO
Page 116 Telegraph Hill from Stockton and
          California streets, 1856
Page 118 Lillie Hitchcock Coit in her firefighting
          youth
Page 118 Coit Tower

WALK THREE
Page 122 Hotaling's whiskey warehouse
Page 124 Transamerica Pyramid and buildings that date from the Gold Rush
Page 126 1856 view of Portsmouth Square
Page 127 Portsmouth Square as it appears today

WALK FOUR
Page 131 Looking up Powell Street at the summit of Nob Hill
Page 133 The Big Four: Mark Hopkins, Collis P. Huntington, Charles Crocker, Leland Stanford
Page 134 The Stanford mansion and the Mark Hopkins castle
Page 135 The Silver Barons: John W. MacKay, James Flood, William S. O'Brien, and James G. Flair
Page 137 The Flood mansion
Page 139 Grace Cathedral
Page 140 Fairmont Hotel
Page 142 Where the cables cross at Powell and California

WALK FIVE
Page 144 Fisherman's Wharf of San Francisco sign
Page 147 Boats in the basin at Fisherman's Wharf
Page 149 View of the Hyde Street Pier and the *Balclutha*

Page 151 William Ralston
Page 153 First map of the Bay made in 1775

Selected Bibliography

Bailey, Paul. *Sam Brannan and the California Mormons.* Los Angeles: Westernlore Press, 1942.

Beck, Warren A., and Williams, David A. *California: A History of the Golden State.* Garden City, NY: Doubleday & Co., 1972.

Billeb, Emil W. *Mining Camp Days.* Berkeley, CA: Howell-North Books, 1968.

Block, Eugene B. *The Immortal San Franciscans for Whom the Streets Were Named.* San Francisco: Chronicle Books, 1971.

Bronson, William. *The Earth Shook, The Sky Burned.* San Francisco: Chronicle Books, 1986.

Cleland, Robert Glass. *A History of California: The American Period.* New York: The MacMillan Co., 1926.

Coit, Margaret L., and editors. *Life History of the United States, Volume 4, The Sweep Westward.* New York: Time, Inc., 1963.

Cole, Tom. *A Short History of San Francisco.* San Francisco: Don't Call it Frisco Press, 1986.

Delehanty, Randolph. *The Ultimate Guide: San Francisco.* San Francisco: Chronicle Books, 1989.

Dickson, Samuel. *The Streets of San Francisco.* Stanford, CA: Stanford University Press, 1947.

Dickson, Samuel. *Tales of San Francisco.* Stanford, CA: Stanford University Press, 1947.

Dillon, Richard H. *San Francisco: Adventurers and Visionaries.* Tulsa, OK: Continental Heritage Press, Inc., 1983.

Eldredge, Zoeth Skinner. *History of California.* New York: The Century History Company, 1915.

Gilliam, Harold. *The Face of San Francisco.* Garden City, NY: Doubleday, 1960.

Hansen, Gladys, and Condon, Emmet. *Denial of Disaster: The Untold Story and Photographs of the San Francisco Earthquake and Fire of 1906.* San Franciso: Cameron and Company, 1989.

Hansen, Gladys. *San Francisco Almanac.* San Francisco: Chronicle Books, 1975.

James, George Wharton. *The Old Franciscan Missions of California.* Boston: Little, Brown, & Co., 1925

Johnson, William Weber. *The Forty-Niners.* New York: Time-Life Books, 1974.

Kahn, Edgar M. *Cabel Car Days in San Francisco.* Stanford, CA: Stanford University Press, 1940.

Lesley, Lewis Burt. *Uncle Sam's Camels: The Journal of May Humphreys Stacy, Supplemented by the Report of Edward Fitzgerald Beale, 1857-1858.* Cambridge, MA: Harvard University Press, 1929.

Lewis, Oscar, and Hall, Carroll D. *Bonanza Inn: America's First Luxury Hotel.* New York: Alfred Knopf, 1939.

Lewis, Oscar. *Sutter's Fort: Gateway to the Gold Fields.* Englewood Cliffs, NJ: Prentice-Hall, Inc., 1966.

Lewis, Oscar. *This Was San Francisco.* New York: David McKay Company, Inc., 1962.

Mayer, Robert. *San Franciso: Chronological & Documentary History, 1542-1970.* Dobbs Ferry, NY: Oceana Publications, 1974.

✓ Muscatine, Doris. *Old San Francisco, The Biography of a City.* New York: G. P. Putnam's Sons, 1975.

Neville, Amelia Ransome. *The Fantastic City.* Cambridge, MA: The Riverside Press, 1932.

Ristow, William. *San Francisco Free and Easy.* San Francisco: Downwind Publications, 1980.

Royce, Josiah. *California: A Study of American Character.* New York: Alfred A. Knopf, 1948.

Scherer, James A. B. *Thirty-first Star.* New York: G. P. Putnam's Sons, 1942.

Soule, Frank. *The Annals of San Francisco.* New York: D. Appleton & Co., 1855.

✓ Starr, Kevin. *Americans and the California Dream 1850-1915.* New York: Oxford University Press, 1973.

Stewart, George R. *Committee of Vigilance, Revolution in San Francisco, 1851.* Boston, MA: Houghton Mifflin, 1964.

Taylor, Bayard. *Eldorado, or Adventures in the Path of Empire.* New York: Stein & Day, 1971.

Wilson, Katherine. *Golden Gate: The Park of a Thousand Vistas.* Caldwell, Idaho: Caxton Printers, Ltd., 1950.

INDEX

1909 Commission 107

A
A. N. Towne mansion 104
Admission to the Union 51, 54, 55
Alioto's 146
Alcalde 15, 21, 58
Alcatraz Island 8
Alhambra 58
Alta California 4, 7, 9, 11, 13, 15, 21, 23
Alta California 67, 69
American River 43, 44
Americans 22-40
Angel Island 8
Annals of San Francisco 26, 39, 42, 55, 56, 81, 115
Anza, Captain Juan Bautista de 9, 11
Aquatic Park 144
Argonauts 46
Argüello, Don Luís Antonio 12, 14, 15
Atherton, Gertrude 14, 107
Australians 68
Ayala, Lieutenant Juan Manuel de 7, 8, 152, 153

B
Baker, Colonel Edward Dickenson 63-65, 128
Balclutha 148-150
Baldwin, Joseph Glover 58

Bank of California 151
Bartlett, Washington A. 31, 33, 42
Bay Area fisheries 148
Beale, Lieutenant Edward F. 38, 39, 46
Bear Flag Revolt 27, 29
Beechey, Captain Frederick William 14
Benton, Senator Thomas Hart 23
Berdue, Thomas 68, 69, 72
Berryessa, Ramon 29
Big Bonanza 136
Big Four 132, 133, 138
Blossom 14
Bluxome, Isaac 73
Brannan, Sam 41-43, 70, 80, 123, 128
Brenham, Charles 72, 73
British 13, 14, 18, 21
Broadway Pier 19
Broderick, David 61-63, 65, 128
Broderick-Terry duel 62
Brooklyn 41, 42, 128
Brown, John Henry 21, 49, 67
Bryant, Edwin 33
Bucareli y Ursua, Lieutenant General Baylio Fray Don Antonio María 9

C
C. A. Thayer 148, 150
Cable cars 50, 110, 130, 132, 141, 142
Cabrillo, Juan Rodrigues 3, 6, 8
Cahuenga Capitulation 39, 40
California Constitutional Convention 24

California Republic 28
California Star 42, 43, 128
California state flag 28
California Street Hill 130, 131
Calistoga 80
Camel Corps 45, 46
Camp Richmond 102
Cañizares, José de 8, 152, 153
The Cannery 144, 148
Cape Horn 46
Carson, Kit 22, 29, 38
Caruso, Enrico 86, 102
Casey, James P. 75, 77-79, 124
Castagnola's 146
Castro district 104
Castro, Isidro de 37
Castro, José 37
Central Emergency Hospital 86
Central Pacific Railroad 132, 133
Chinatown 20
City Christmas tree 112
City Hall 88, 86
Clark, William Squire 49, 121
Clark's Point 49, 144
Clay Compromise 55
Clay, Senator Henry 54, 55
Cleaning Day 102
Cleland, Robert 48
Cobweb Palace 145
Coffin, George 58
Cogswell, Dr. Henry 115

Coit, Lillie Hitchcock 107, 117-119
Coit Tower 115, 117-119
Cole, R. Beverly 79
Coleman, William T. 69, 70, 73, 75, 77, 79
Colton, David 138
Colton, Walter 44
Committee of Fifty 89, 128
Committee of Vigilance 65, 70, 72-74, 128
Comstock Lode 151
Concepción 14, 15
Congress 39
Convention delegates 53
Cora, Charles 74, 77, 78, 79
Corruption 51
Crabtree, Lotta 110, 123
Crespi, Father Juan 4
Criminals 68
Crocker, Charles 104, 132, 133, 138, 139
Crocker, William H. 104
Customs House 70, 128
Cyane 37

D
Dana, Richard Henry 22, 148
Davis, Jefferson 45
Davis, William Heath 18
De Haro, Francisco 12, 15, 21, 29
Delmonico's Restaurant 89, 90
De Neve, Felipe 11
Dewey Monument 91, 112, 113
Discovery 13

Dolores Park 96, 97, 104
Dolphin Club 150
Donahue, Peter 110
Donner Party 46, 48
Downey, Joseph 29, 42, 121
Drake, Francis 1, 3, 8
DuPont, Samuel F. 39

E
Earthquakes 60, 81-107
Eddy, William M. 24, 34, 48
Ellis, Alfred J. 54, 73, 76
Embarcadero 50
Euphemia 57, 67, 121
Eureka 148, 150
Evening Bulletin 75, 79, 119
Examiner 102
Explorers 1-8

F
Fair, James 140
Fairmont Hotel 103, 104, 140, 141
The Fantastic City 108
Farallon Islands 1, 3
Ferry Building 89, 108, 109
Ferryboat Era 108
Field, Charles 122
Fifty Vara survey 20
Fillmore, President Millard 55
Fire department 84
Fire Department Museum 58, 104
Fires 58, 69, 84
First house, 16
First Unitarian Church 65

Fisherman's Grotto 146
Fisherman's Wharf 144-147
Flair, James G. 135, 136
Fletc, Francis 1
Flood, James 135-138, 140
Flood mansion 103, 104, 136, 137, 140
Folsom, Captain Joseph L. 26
Font, Father Pedro 11, 12
Fort Bragg 3
Fort Gunnybags 75-78
Fort Mason 95, 144
Freemasonry 123
Fremont, Jessie Benton 23, 64
Fremont, Major John C. 22, 23, 27, 29, 32, 37, 39
Funston, General Frederick 84, 89, 95, 97, 102

G
Gálvez, José de 4, 8
Gambling houses 51, 57
Geary, John White 56, 57, 61, 69, 113, 121
Geddis, Paul 56
Genthe, Arnold 102
Ghirardelli 154
Ghirardelli Chocolate factory 121
Ghirardelli Square 144, 154
Gold 41-51, 53
Gold Hydrant 60, 95, 104
Gold Rush 19, 36, 44, 48, 67, 80
Golden Era 29, 121
Golden Gate 23
Golden Gate Park 104

Golden Hinde 1, 8
Gough, Charles 55
Gough, Octavia 55
Grace Cathedral 104, 139
Grand Hotel 86
Grant Avenue 19, 20
Gray, George & Harry 117
Great Fire 92, 97
Great Pacificator 54
Green, Talbot 56
Guerrero, Francisco 21

H
Haggin, James Ben Ali 132
Haight, Henry 73
Hall of Justice 69, 128
Halleck, Henry W. 53, 54, 124
Hallidie, Andrew 130
Ham and Eggs Fire 86, 89
Harte, Bret 14, 123
Hays, Sheriff John 72
Hayes Valley, 86
Hinckley, Captain William 21, 29
History of California, 48
Hopkins, Mark 132, 133, 141
Hopkins, Sterling 79
Horse-drawn fire engine 93
Hotaling's whiskey warehouse 122
The Hounds 67, 68
Howard, William D. M. 18, 19, 31, 49,
    73, 125
Hudson's Bay Company 18, 125
Hundred Vara survey 20
Huntington, Collis P. 132, 133, 138

Huntington Hotel 138
Huntington Park 138
Hyde, George 49, 50, 110
Hyde Street Pier 148, 149

I
Ide, William B. 28
Inner Signal Station 115
Italian Fisherman's Association 145

J
Jack's Restaurant 67
Jackson, President 23
Jackson Square, 97
Jail 51, 57, 67
Jansen, Charles J. 68, 73
Jenkins, John 70, 72, 128
Johnson, Governor J. Neely 77, 79
Jones, Elbert P. 42, 49
Jones, Thomas Ap Catesby 23
Judah, Theodore 133
Julia 79

K
Kearny, Major General Stephen Watts
    36, 38, 39, 45
Kemble, Edward 42, 43
King, Thomas Starr 64, 65
King of William, James 74, 75, 77, 79,
    124
Kipling, Rudyard 141, 142

L
Landfilling operations 81

Larkin, Thomas 47, 53
Law and Order Party 76, 77
Leavenworth, Thaddeus 51, 57
Leese, Jacob P. 16-18, 44, 73, 125
Leese, Rosalia 16
Leidesdorff, William 25, 49
Lick, James 154
Lincoln, Abraham 63
Little Chile 67
Lotta's Fountain 104, 110, 111

M
MacKay, John W. 135, 136
Made ground 81
Maiden Lane 112
Mail 56
Manifest Destiny 22, 23
Mark Hopkins castle 134
Mark Hopkins Hotel 104, 134
Mark Hopkins Institute of Art 104
Market Street 33, 51
Marshall, James 43, 80
Martin, Leonard 148
Martínez, Ignacio 15, 21
Martínez, María 15
Mason, Colonel Richard B. 44-46, 49,
    123
Masonic Auditorium, 104
McAllister, Hall 68, 69, 73
McKenzie, Robert 72
Mechanic's Library 73
Mechanics' Pavilion 86, 125
Meiggs, Henry 145
Meiggs' Wharf 145

Mellus, Henry 19, 73, 125
Merritt, Ezekiel 27
Mexican-American War 40
Mexicans 16, 21, 23, 24
Mexico 23, 28
Minerva 52
Mission Bay 97
Mission District 95
Mission Dolores 11-13, 26, 51
Mission Dolores Park 95
Mission San Francisco de Asís 11
Missions 4
Moncada, Captain Fernando de Rivera y 4, 8
Monterey 9, 11, 23, 24, 44
Monterey Bay, 3, 6, 29
Montgomery, Captain John B. 29-31, 39, 41, 121, 125, 128, 152
Montgomery Block 86, 87, 97, 124, 125
Moraga, Lieutenant José Joaquín 11, 21
Mormons 41, 42
Morton Street 111
Moscone, Mayor 102
Mulford, Prentice 77
Municipal taxation 51
Municipal court 57

N
Name changed 31
National Maritime Museum 144, 152
Natoma Street 19
Neville, Amelia Ransome 108, 111, 132
New Helvetia 47
Newton, Frederick 122

Nob Hill 89, 104, 107, 130-132, 135
Noé, José de Jesús 21, 31
North Beach 95, 115, 144
Norton the First, Emperor 112, 113

O
O'Brien, William S. 135, 136
O'Farrell, Jasper 31-33, 34, 44, 110
O'Farrell's 1847 Survey 33, 39, 83, 123
Official seal 59
Oregon 55
Orion 15
Ortega, Sergeant José Francisco de 7, 8

P
Pacific Union Club 104, 135
Palace Hotel 86, 97, 104, 105, 107, 119, 151, 152
Palou, Father Francisco 6, 8, 11
Pico, General Pio 23, 37, 38
Pierce, President Franklin 55, 79
Police force 51, 57, 67
Polk, Willis 135
Polk, President 23, 39, 45
Pony Express 128
Portals of the Past 107
Porter, David 46
Portolá, Captain Gaspar de 4, 6-8, 11
Portsmouth House Hotel 21, 67
Portsmouth Square 19, 21, 42, 58, 62, 69, 70, 121, 126-128
Preble, 89
Prentice Mulford's Story 77
Presidio 12-15, 19, 95

Punta de los Reyes (Point Reyes) 7

R
Rae, William Glen 18
Ralston, William 86, 151
Regulators 67
Reminiscences 21
Rezanov, Nikolai Petrovich 14, 15
Richardson, William 15, 16, 24, 74
Richmond district, 104
Ridley, Robert 20, 29, 30
Russailh, Albert Benard de 66
Russian Hill 97
Russians 3, 9, 14

S
Sabella and La Torre 146
Sacramento 47, 48
San Antonio 4
San Carlos 4, 6, 8, 152, 153
San Francisco Bay 6, 7, 11, 15, 18, 41, 42
San Francisco Mint 97, 104
Schmitz, Mayor 89, 95, 128
Second Committee of Vigilance 74-76, 79
Semple, Robert 28
Serra, Father Junípero 4, 7
Settlers 9-21
Seward, W. H. 110
Sheraton Palace Hotel 104, 106
Sherman, William Tecumseh 123
Sidewalks 32, 51, 60, 139
Sydney Ducks 68, 69

Silver Barons 135
Sloat, John D. 29
Slocum, General 95
South End Rowing Club 150
Spain 3, 15
Spanish 9, 13, 14
Spear, Nathan 18
St. Francis Hotel 119
Stanford Court Hotel 132
Stanford, Leland 132, 133, 141
Stanford mansion 104, 132, 134
Statehood 52-65
Stevenson, Robert Louis 128
Stockton, General Robert F. 31, 37-39
Strauss, Levi 49
Street maintenance 51
Street of the Founding 19
Street Walk One 108-114
Street Walk Two 115-120
Street Walk Three 121-129
Street Walk Four 130-143
Street Walk Five 144-155
Street widths 20
Stuart, James 68, 72
Sullivan, Dennis 84
Sutro, Adolph 86, 124, 125
Sutter, John 43, 47, 48, 53, 80
Sutter's Fort 43, 47, 48

T
Tarantino's 146
Taraval, Sebastian 11
Tavernier, Jules 123
Telegraph 117

Telegraph Hill 31, 97, 115-117, 145
Terry, David S. 61, 62, 79
Tetrazzini, Luisa 111
Tobin, Richard 132
Todd, Frank Morton 115
Town's name 42
Townsend, John 51
Transamerica Pyramid 36, 122, 124, 125
Treaty of Guadalupe Hidalgo 40, 53
Truett, Miers F. 77
Twain, Mark 44, 123
Two Years Before the Mast 22, 148

U
U.S. Post Office 97
U.S.S. *Portsmouth* 29, 35, 121, 152
Union Oil Building, 70
Union Square 61, 89, 91, 113

V
Vaillancourt Fountain 110
Valencia Street Hotel 83
Vallejo, General Mariano Guadalupe 16, 21, 27, 29
Vallejo, Rosa 16
Vancouver, George 13, 14, 18
Vandalia 35
Van Ness, James 77
Vigilantes 66-80
Vioget, Jean Jaques 19, 32
Vioget survey 19, 20, 32, 128
Viscaino, Sebastian 6

W
Warner, Abe 145
Water lots 33
Washington Square 115
Webster, Daniel 54, 55
Western Addition 24, 55, 95
What Cheer House 25
Wilde, Oscar 123
Windred, Robert 68, 69
Wittaker, Samuel 72
Wittmer, Jacob 43
Women's property 54
Woodward, R. B. 25

Y
Yerba Buena, 15, 16, 18-21, 29, 30, 41, 121
Yerba Buena Cove 19, 36, 44, 48, 57, 110, 121, 125, 144
Yerba Buena Island 8, 15
Yerba Buena's first baby 16
Yerba Buena's first wharf 49
Young, Brigham 41
Yung, Nicholas 138, 140